Granny D's Day Hikers Guide to Democracy

Words of Doris
"Granny D" Haddock
from her pro-democracy
walks across America

Copyright © 2019 Dennis Michael Burke

All rights reserved. Permission to quote from individual speeches or to reproduce up to six speeches in whole is hereby granted. More information: Info@lenfantpress.com L'Enfant Press, Washington D.C. This book is an abridgement of "Democracy Road, the Speeches of Doris 'Granny D' Haddock."

Front cover oil portrait by Karin Wells of Peterborough, New Hampshire; copyright the artist
Back cover photo by Julie Broxton

ISBN: 978-1-7345867-2-5

Sen. John McCain:

"Granny D, you exceed any small, modest contributions those of us who have labored in the vineyards of reform have made to this Earth."

Jimmy Carter:

"Doris Haddock is a true patriot, and our nation has been blessed by her remarkable life."

Molly Ivins:

"The problem with Granny D is that she makes the rest of us look like such schlumps."

Bill Moyers:

"John McCain and Bill Bradley were looking over her shoulder, reading her speeches and watching how she succeeded in making campaign finance reform an emotional and patriotic issue with many Americans. When presidential candidate Al Gore finally signed-on to campaign finance reform, his speech cited McCain, Bradley and Doris Haddock."

It happens quickly

and moves swiftly. It is nothing for the forces of raw power to discredit the proper law enforcement agencies and set up new ones run by political cronies, with prisons and police of their own to suppress and arrest those who dare investigate or protest. It is nothing for raw power to thumb its nose at the interests of world peace or the Earth's environment for the sake of power and plunder. It can happen quickly. It can happen in America. We must have our eyes open for it and our voices ready!

Those who speak out first—the leakers, whistleblowers, activists, patriots—will be vilified, jailed, or worse. Stick up for them. Oppose the autocrat at every turn. You will be among a new generation of American patriots putting yourselves at risk to preserve our dream of individual and civic freedom. Nothing is more important than this work, as the history of the previous century shows us— clearly written as it is in the blood of one hundred million people.

To those who died for democracy we owe a sacred trust. For those who died for lack of democracy we owe our efforts to make a world worthy of their memory. Democracy is worth a great deal of trouble and all our human strength.

—Doris Haddock's remarks in Florida, June 16, 2001, to a voter rights meeting of young activists in Tallahassee

Contents

Note from New Hampshire 7
Note from the Family 8
About Doris 9
The Center of the World 13
The Road So Far 15
Together at the Table of Power 25
To the Apologists of Corruption 32
Your Answer, Mr. McConnell 34
A Brisk Walk Across the Country 37
Our Town 38
The Efficacy of Sacrifice 42
A Modest Proposal for Sacrifice 45
The Disruption Economy 48
Don't Give Up the Ship 51
Entering Washington, D.C. 56
On the U.S. Capitol Steps 57
Taxation Without Representation 61
Good to be Home 64
We Are Problem-Solvers 66
Her remarks inside the Capitol Rotunda 69
The Seven-Layer Cake 73
The Bribery Coast 76
Corporate Leadership 78
Freedom from Anger 82
This, My Government 84
The Monster at the Door 94
Old Elijah's Tree 96
The Road to Freedom 99
Fight Like Hell 101
Be Open to Your Own Genius 106

How the Takeover Artists Took Over 108
What We are *For* 115
Trust Your Own Values 119
Back at Harvard 123
Let's Talk About You 131
I Walked—Now I'll Run 134
The Five Nations 137
In Faneuil Hall 142
Reorganize the Democratic Party 145
Why Facts Don't Matter to Our Opposition 148
Last Delivered Speech 156
The Swamp to Drain is Anger (undelivered) 157
Senator Russ Feingold, Senate Floor, Oct. 14, 1999 162
.... 164

Note from New Hampshire

We find ourselves living in a time of existential crisis for our democracy. We need to inspire each other to summon the creative energy needed to meet this challenge. Please let Doris's words—her bold speeches and little whispers—help inspire you to keep at it. We know that each of us *can* make an important difference.

Doris showed us how it's done. She fought against the bully of big money politics. She fought against authoritarianism, which means she fought for our freedoms, which all depend upon the rule of law applied without political influence. She fought for the survival of a livable planet. She fought of the rights of all groups among us; she fought for love and against fear.

She lost some battles but never the war, as her central intention was to raise awareness and promote values—those long-term shapers of policy and culture. And that, she did.

She made extraordinary efforts for her grandchildren and for me and you, just as I now must carry on for my daughter, Ellie, and as you carry on for the world you hope to shape. We do this for each other and for people we will never meet and for generations to come. That is our central intention.

The late Ruth Bader Ginsburg said, "Fight for the things that you care about, but do it in a way that will lead others to join you." Remember that Doris began her walk across the nation with just herself and a volunteer or two, but arrived in Washington, D.C. with over two thousand. Her model of organizing was sacrifice. It works. Let's remember that.

Olivia Zink. Executive Director
Coalition for Open Democracy, Concord, New Hampshire
(Doris Haddock's legacy organization,
OpenDemocracyNH.org)

Note from the Family

I knew Doris for 52 years. She was the best mother-in-law that any young wife could wish for. In October of 1960 I married her only son, Jim, in his junior year at Springfield College. Doris knew we had no money to speak of, so she took it upon herself to make my clothes. She always let me pick out the material and the patterns—she even made my winter coat!

She would get up at 5:30, make a quick breakfast, then go off to work as an executive at a shoe company. I believe that she was the best-paid woman in Manchester, New Hampshire at the time.

After work she would make supper and then go about making my clothes or new dresses for her own daughter or her granddaughters. She would, like a little factory, continuously knit sweaters, hats, scarves and mittens. She hooked rugs as a fundraiser for Native American communities in Arizona.

She had the ability to focus her efforts in a way that I had not witnessed before—with the exception of her son, Jim. My Father always said Jim could accomplish in one day what it would take a week for ten men.

I watched Doris take on cause after cause. The first was in 1959, when she worked to stop the Atomic Energy Commission from blasting an artificial harbor in the Alaska coast with a hydrogen bomb. The village of Point Hope was located there and was the home of the oldest indigenous Eskimo people in Alaska. Strontium-90 would have spread over the tundra for a great distance—the Caribou eat the tundra grass and the Eskimos eat the Caribou. They would have been wiped out. Doris and her husband battled this for two years, and they won, stopping the H-bomb and saving the village. The people of the village became her lifelong friends.

She stopped a proposed highway from destroying one of the most beautiful towns in New England. She did not like being perceived as a pariah, but she was intent on preserving the town, and she did.

She was every day a force to behold. People who knew her have not forgotten her. Quite regularly a walk is held throughout New Hampshire to remember her and to remind people (including visiting presidential candidates) of our ever more desperate need for campaign finance reform.

Elizabeth "Libby" Haddock

About Doris

By her own reckoning, Doris Haddock, 1910-2010, was the usual sort of New Englander: a bit flinty, persevering, practical to a fault, hardly special. She wrote thank you notes almost continuously. On New Year's Day, 1999, 24 days before her 90th birthday, she began her walk from California to Washington, D.C. to promote political reform—specifically campaign finance reform (the attempt to get big, special-interest dollars out of politics). She had hitchhiked around New Hampshire and camped on the ground to prepare for the 3,200-mile walk, which, despite her

arthritis, emphysema and a bad back, was accomplished by walking ten miles a day for a year and two months. She took a few hitchhiking detours along the way in order to make speeches off the trail or to arm-twist members of Congress and presidential candidates.

She made hundreds of speeches, many of them extemporaneous to small groups in tiny city halls and living rooms; she often drew a diagram to show the flow of money from corporations and wealthy donors to politicians, and the resulting flow of tax breaks, environmental loopholes and other public benefits to the donors in repayment—a system costing taxpayers $10 for every campaign dollar donated. The innate corruption of the system is well known now, but it was not so when she began her one-woman education of America.

She became interested in campaign finance reform in the mid-1990s, mainly through her New Hampshire women's book club and study group—the Tuesday Morning Academy, as they called themselves. It became clear to them that American democracy was being rapidly undermined by the quid pro quo of large political donations from corporations and billionaires. Oligarchy was rapidly displacing America's governance of, by, and for the people.

On January 1, 1999, soon to be age 89, Granny D—as she was

called by her grandchildren and soon by millions of others—boarded a plane to California, where she began a 3,200-mile walk to Washington. She did so in order to demonstrate her concern for the issue and, as she hoped, to drum-up popular support for a campaign finance reform bill. She did achieve that—it passed Congress and was signed into law. According to the bill's two

Republican and two Democrat sponsors, it would not have passed without her sacrificial show of concern, which engaged the conscience of a nation.

> "I was still something of a desperado in those first months of the walk—roaming over the dry and blank space remaining at the end of a life. Or was it the lull between acts? Who can ever know at such times? There is an urge to just walk into the desert, away from the road and be done with it. There is also an urge to have some ice cream with chocolate sauce. Life is what we patch together between those competing desires." —from her first memoir

She walked for fourteen months, speaking to people individually and in town audiences along the way. She hiked across deserts and climbed the Appalachian Range in blizzard conditions. Over 2,200 supporters gathered to walk the last miles with her to the Capitol Building, including a dozen or more Members of Congress and live crews from Good Morning America, the Today show, and television crews from Japan, Germany and the UK.

The marchers—with reform hero Jim Hightower leading chants with his megaphone—made a big noise down K Street's lobbyist row and then swarmed the Capitol grounds. Though a permit for only 100 people had been allowed, she arrived with several thousand. The Capitol Police threw up their hands and let them pass onto the grounds. Her remarks on the Capitol steps, with Members of Congress all around her, have been taught in university rhetoric courses.

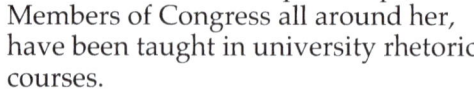

It took two more years after her walk to gain Congressional passage of the reform bill, during which time she engaged in a four-day, 24-hour walking fast around the Capitol Building in the snow, rallies in many states, and demonstrations in the Capitol Rotunda that twice landed her in jail. She conducted her own filibuster in the U.S. Capitol office of a corrupt congressman, reading from his list of compromising corporate contributions until she was removed. Through it all, she generated a flood of calls and messages to Congress.

When the bill did pass Congress (though it was later undermined by the Supreme Court's Citizens United decision), the sponsors, including Senators McCain and Feingold, and U.S. Representatives Shays and Meehan, credited Doris Haddock from the floors if the Senate and House with raising public awareness of the crisis in a way that finally allowed the bill to pass.

It passed the House late at night. The sponsors then walked out of the building into the dark with Doris, who had watched from the gallery as they voted and as Mr. Gephardt and others looked up to her and saluted.

Since her walk, campaign finance reform, though it has taken a serious but hardly permanent hit from the Supreme Court, has remained high on the list of changes demanded by democracy advocates of all parties. Her words are often quoted in that work, and many states have enacted reforms as a result of her visits and encouragement. Presidential candidates, especially when visiting New Hampshire, cite her as the embodiment of American democratic reform.

Doris was born on January 24, 1910 in Laconia, New Hampshire. She attended Emerson College for three years before being ejected for the offense of getting married. She was, however, awarded an honorary degree from the college in 2000, and to standing cheers.

She nursed her husband through ten years of Alzheimer's disease. After his death in 1998, and then after the death of her closest woman friend, Elizabeth Foster, of Dundee, she picked herself up and started planning her walk for campaign reform.

In 2010, Doris Haddock died in her son and daughter-in-law's forest home at age 100. A week before her death she was still walking five miles a day and writing thank you notes to compatriots and letters of demand to politicians.

She left as her legacy to us the essential democratic gift of civic encouragement. "Democracy is not something we have, it's something we do," is a quote she loved.

When Doris was nearing the completion of her long walk, the worst snowstorm in forty years buried the roads. She noticed a wide, snowy path that opened in the woods outside Cumberland, Maryland. It was the historic towpath that runs next to the C&O Canal.

"How long is it?" she asked a park ranger, who had just chained off the entrance because the snow was dangerously deep—too deep for hikers.

"Well, ma'am," he said, "it runs for 184 and one-half miles from here all the way into Georgetown, in DC," he said.

"I'll need my cross-country skis," she said.

The park ranger and his supervisor agreed to take their lunch break and look the other way, should someone slip under the chain. After all, the woman was not to be denied on her birthday. She skied the last 184 and one-half miles into Washington.

She didn't fix democracy, but only because democracy is never fixed; it is always just propped up—fought for again, died for again—because the politics of fear and the politics of love are always

pushing against each other in this world, as Doris often reminded us.
And we must have faith in our power to make change, just as she did, especially in this time of danger.

How did she connect with people? Here are some examples:
The people of the little town of Salome, Arizona, on a few hours' notice, organized a makeshift parade for her, led by the town's fire truck, with half the town's kids aboard. After that arrival, she

was hosted at a little reception of cookies and lemonade and was asked why she was walking across America at her age. As she later recalled:
"I simply reminded them that many people died or gave up their sons and daughters for our freedoms, and that we mustn't give it away now to the corruption that has become the normal business of Washington. It was my mention of the wartime sacrifices that made my remarks hit home. That part of the message has always been easy for me, as those laying in rows upon rows in our national cemeteries are the people who come to mind when I think of our duty to preserve our freedoms—and we are not free if we do not have control of our representatives."—From a draft of her first memoir.

And here is another memory:
"By the time we got to Tombstone it was just Matt [Keller] and me. We walked along the covered wooden sidewalks of the old town, past the real OK Corral, and found the mayor, who was genuinely delighted to meet me, even without network news in tow. He gave me a key to the city and a nice certificate and showed us around. Later, we tried to buy an ice cream cone at the Bird Cage Theater, but our money was no good anywhere in town. So, we took our free ice cream and sat on a bench on the sidewalk. A beautiful dark-haired, dark-eyed, woman, the owner of the Silver Nugget Saloon, took us out that night to her Silver Nugget for a drink, then to a nearby steakhouse for a Western dinner, and finally to Big Nose Kate's for a nightcap. Well, that's why they put rails along the sidewalks in Western towns like that—not just for the horses. At Big Nose Kate's, (she) commanded the guitar-strumming cowboy to serenade me, which he did. A few rounds later, she had a tug-of-war with a cowboy poet over the microphone, both of them frothing with wonderful verse. And they had to hear from me. Well, everybody in Big Nose Kate's knows everything about Campaign Finance Reform now. You just go check and see if I didn't make them experts, if they remember anything at all."

The Center of the World

> *Friday evening, May 14, 1999 at the Rodeo Arena in Pecos, Texas: Ms. Haddock was a guest speaker at an all-night walk around the arena to raise funds for cancer research. She had walked through California, Arizona, New Mexico and Texas west of the Pecos.*

Thank you very much. I am honored to be here in Pecos. I began my walk to Washington D.C. from Los Angeles some 1,200 miles ago, and all of those miles have been walked in a place described by earlier generations of Americans as the land west of the Pecos. On Sunday, I will wade across the Pecos and enter the other half of creation. But tonight, I am here at the center of the world and am proud to meet all of you who live here.

I thank you for having me here on such a beautiful evening. Life is a beautiful experience, and here we all are together, alive at this moment, breathing the same cool air. The issue that brings everyone here tonight is a terrible disease, of course, and we Americans fight it because we naturally rise to the fight against any evil that threatens those we love.

Deep inside, we can be joyful to remember that nobody really dies in this great drama of the soul we live in eternally. Some of us move on faster than others, and we so deeply miss those who have left this stage before us. Tonight, we see that there is something we can do with that loneliness and pain.

When my husband died several years ago, and when my best friend, Elizabeth, died last year, I looked at my life and my lifelong beliefs and said to myself, what shall I do now? What can I do to honor the memory of the people I have loved? How can I turn my pain into something beautiful in the world? Something beautiful? Let me tell you that great art and great writing often is the tricking of suffering into beauty. Life is full of suffering; what we must do when we have more than we can bear is to transform it into beauty through a medium of exchange such as art, or handiwork, or a written story or poem, or good parenting, or good friendship, or the creation of good work in the community, or the pursuit of some work we may find unfinished among our lifelong interests and concerns—some in the attic too long. So, I asked myself, what work can I do that may be done as a memorial to those I miss? What can I do to amaze them as they watch lovingly from the other side?

And so, if you are here because you are remembering someone lost, you are turning that loss into the art of this special evening we are sharing together. And if you are here to pursue your own battle with a dangerous disease, or to give emotional support to someone you love who is doing that or who has lost someone, then you are a part of that creative transformation of pain into beauty. What is more beautiful than people warmly sharing an evening together in the glow of candles? What is more emotionally healing?

The issue that I decided to do something about as a memorial to the people I loved and still love is political reform of our elections. It is, of course, a fool's errand. It is just an old woman walking across the land, wearing my late friend

Elizabeth's gardening hat, until it recently fell to tatters, talking to whomever will listen about the kind of political reforms most people don't believe can really happen.

Also, there are two things I would like you to understand about impossible missions. One is the fact that, sometimes, *all you can do* is put your body in front of a problem and stand there as a witness to it. That is part of healing because it is not denial of the problem, and our individual conscious mind is part of the larger conscious mind of society. What you think and how you think does affect the world, and your actions do matter.

Never be discouraged from being an activist because people might tell you that you'll not succeed. You have already succeeded if you're out there representing truth or justice or compassion or fairness or love. You already have your victory because you have changed the world; you have changed the status quo by you; you have changed the chemistry of things and changes will spread from you, will be easier to happen again in others because of you, because, believe it or not, you are the center of the world.

There is a second thing you need to know about impossible causes, which is that there are no impossible causes on this Earth, if they are good causes. We can do nearly anything together, and we really do remarkable things. We will cure cancer most certainly because people like you walk through the night to make it so. We have nearly eradicated polio worldwide; we have actually cured smallpox; we are curing many diseases—impossible dreams but a short time ago.

My dream of political reform will come true. I may live to see it from this side of life, or I will smile to see it from the other side. But it will happen. It will happen because people love this country and this democracy, and because they have given their sons and daughters and the best years of their own lives to defend it. They will not let it be destroyed before their eyes by these obscene floods of special-interest money that come into our elections from big business and the very rich. I know we will end that outrage and we will be able to run our communities and our nation to look after the interests of the common people, for that is what a democracy is all about.

I wish all of you good health. I wish you the courage to live out your emotions and your beliefs in your daily lives, as you are doing tonight. I admire you all tremendously, and I will always remember this evening at the great center of our beautiful world.

The Road So Far

> *In Texas, Ms. Haddock's trek was the subject of regular coverage by Jim Hightower's progressive radio show, based in Austin. He called her nearly every morning and interviewed her as she walked. This brought her to the attention of Ross Perot. Though not a member of Perot's Reform Party, and not in line with much of its philosophy, Doris was invited by Mr. Perot to address his party's national convention in Dearborn, July 23, 1999. She gave two speeches there, as the Party had split into two and was meeting separately. Both gave standing, shouting ovations, and one groups, in fun, nominated her for the vice presidency of the United States. She declined.*

There are always a few questions about whom I am and what I hope to accomplish by walking from the Pacific to the Atlantic at the age of 89. Who I am is an old reformer, and I feel at home in this room. *A great and sustained cheer arose.]* I have been involved in reform fights through most of my adult life, but I have saved the most important for my last hurrah.

It is my belief that every American ought to be able to run for a public office without having to sell his or her soul.

Fundraising muscle should not be the measure of a candidate. Ideas, character, track record, leadership skills: these ought to be the measures of our leaders.

The hundreds of thousands of our dead, buried in rows upon rows in our national cemeteries, sacrificed their lives for the democracy of a free people, not for what we have today. It is up to each of us to see that these boys and girls did not die in vain.

With the support of my dear children, grandchildren and great grandchildren, I began my trek and I will see it through. I am doing it to bring attention to the fact that ordinary Americans like me care desperately about the condition of our government and the need for campaign finance reform.

I have traveled as a pilgrim, and Americans have taken care of me through each of my 1,800 miles so far. If you knew, as I know from these last seven months, what a sweet and decent nation we live in, you would be all the more determined to raise it out of this time of trouble, this sewer of greed and cash that we have slipped into.

Ladies and gentlemen, I have come quite a way across our land, looking at every inch and meeting everyone I can.

Please imagine that you have sent me out to walk across America so that I might, this evening, report to you some findings to help you in your deliberations.

Friends, I have walked through a land where the middle class, the foundation of our democracy, stands nearly in ruins.

Main streets have given way to superstores. Towns have died. Family farms, family businesses and local owners have given way to absentee owners and a local population of underpaid clerks and collection agents. People are so stressed in their household economies, and in the personal relationships that depend on family economics, that they have little time for participation in the governance of their communities or of their nation. They struggle daily in mazes and treadmills of corporate design and inhuman intent. They dearly believe their opinions matter, but they don't believe their voices count.

They tell me that the control of their government has been given over to commercial interests. They cheer me on, sometimes in tears, but they wonder if we will ever again be—and, for some, finally be—a self-governing people, a free people.

With the middle class so purposefully destroyed—its assets plundered by an elite minority—it should not surprise us that the war chests of presidential candidates are grotesquely overflowing with cash while children go hungry and elders must eat pet food to survive. I have met these people. The wealth of our nation is now dangerously concentrated. The privileged elite intend to elect those who have helped them achieve this theft and who will help them preserve their position of advantage. That is what accounts for the avalanche of big checks into presidential campaigns.

Walk through this city—Dearborn and Detroit—and mark the doors of the families who cannot afford to give a small fortune to a presidential candidate or a senator or two. For those who live behind these millions of doors, we do not have a democracy, but an emergency—a crisis that deeply threatens our future as a free people.

The thousands of Americans I have met are discouraged, but they are not defeated—nor will they ever be. They know that the government and the social order presently do not represent their interests and are not within their control—that American democracy is nearly a fiction. But the flame of freedom that no longer burns in public, burns securely in their longing.

It is said that democracy is not something we have, but something we do. But right now, we cannot do it because we cannot speak. We are shouted down by the bullhorns of big money. It is money with no manners for democracy, and it must be escorted from the room.

While wealth has always influenced our politics, what is new is the increasing concentration of wealth and the widening divide between the political interests of the common people and the political interests of the very wealthy—who now buy our willing leaders wholesale. The wealthy elite used to steal what they needed, and it hardly affected the rest of us. Now they have the power to take everything for themselves, laying waste to our communities, our culture, our environment and our lives, and they are doing it.

What villainy allows this political condition? It is the combination of two viral ideas: that money is speech and that corporations are people. If money is speech, then those with more money have more speech, and that idea is antithetical to democracy. It makes us no longer equal citizens. This perverse notion, and the general, unrestricted participation of such money in our elections, must be and will be stopped if democracy is to survive. That removal, that riding out of town on a rail, was done a century ago when Republican president Theodore Roosevelt pushed corporate money out of politics. In his absence, and in the absence of backbone in the parties and in the Congress, the slick operators have slinked back into town, and in many cases have been invited back or even coerced back into town by elected leaders who have the gall to think that the democracy our children died for is no more than a dirty bag of barter for their enrichment. They are traitors to everything good that America stands for, and it is time for us to get out that rail again. Here is what Teddy Roosevelt said in 1907:

"...Our government, national and state, must be freed from the sinister influence or control of special interests. Exactly as the special interests of cotton and slavery threatened our political integrity before the Civil War, so now the great special business interests too often control and corrupt the men and methods of government for their own profit. We must drive the special interests out of politics. That is one of our tasks today... The citizens of the United States must effectively control the mighty commercial forces, which they have themselves called into being. There can be no effective control of corporations while their political activity remains. To put an end to it will be neither a short nor an easy task, but it can be done," he said.

Teddy Roosevelt said it well. Business corporations are not people. They are protective associations that we, the people, allow to be chartered for business purposes on the condition that they serve the community and will behave.

We must look to whether we can still afford, as a people and as a planet, to give these little monsters a birth certificate but no proper upbringing, no set of expectations, no consequences for antisocial behavior.

We are simply tired of the damage they do, and we are tired of cleaning up after them. If they are to be allowed to exist—and they are indeed important to us—they must agree to be responsible for their own activities, start to finish, without requiring public dollars to be used to clean their rooms up after them. The era of corporate irresponsibility must be ended immediately, particularly in regard to the degradation of our political and cultural and natural environments, while we still have the power to act. Parents know that there comes a time when infantile behavior persists, but the child is too large to do much with. We Americans still can act in regard to the corporations we have given birth to, but not by much of an advantage. Our advantage will evaporate early in the 21st Century if we do not act soon.

Friends, does it matter if it is Rupert Murdoch or another such, instead of Marshall Tito or Nikita Khrushchev, who owns everything and decides everything for us? The soul of democracy is diversity, not concentration. Diversity requires the human scale, not monstrous scale. It is all quite enough to make us mad, but let me advise you, on the eve of your meetings, that we cannot afford to act out of anger, if we desire to win.

Politics today is quite too characterized by anger and even hatred; so, let's have none of it here.

If you have true enemies in politics, pray that their lives are filled with anger, for no one so filled can win for long. Anger drains your energy and makes you incapable of endurance or of creative leadership. If you win, your victory will be short-lived. Ask the failed leaders of the so-called Republican Revolution if I am right. Negativity is negativity, and it has no place at the helm of a democracy. It doesn't know what to do with power when it gets it. Only joy and optimism—and love, really—can win in the long term because only they can serve.

General Eisenhower said, "Pessimism never won any battle" He was right. Pessimism visualizes defeat. What we visualize, we bring forth. Carl Sandburg wrote: "Nothing happens unless first a dream."

To the reformers, then: learn optimism if you would have the endurance to succeed, and endurance is required.

Where to find optimism? Well, I have found it for you out on the road, and I give it to you now. It is this:

I give you the Americans I have met. Without exception, they deeply love the idea of America. It is an image they carry in their hearts. It is a dream they are willing to sacrifice their lives for. Many of them do. There is no separating this image of democracy from their longing for personal freedom for themselves, their family, their friends. To the extent that our government is not our own, we are not free people. We feel a heavy oppression in our lives because we have lost hold of this thing, this self-governance that is rightfully ours, because it is our dream and our history. But the spirit of freedom is strong in the

American soul, and it is the source of our optimism and joy, because it will always overcome its oppressors.

On the road so far, these Americans have taken me into their homes and fed me at their tables—shown me the children for whom they sacrifice their working lives and for whom they pray for a free and gentle democracy. And I will tell you that I am with them. I am with their dream and I know you are, too. We are all on this road and we must stay on it together, forgetting our minor differences until, together, we achieve the necessary objective of restoring democracy for individuals, and allowing each individual an equal voice in the civil discussions we have as a self-governing people.

We must end our American Century with the optimism and clear purpose and high ideals with which it began. We must visualize this goal clearly, and work to make it so.

Yes, it is a long road ahead. But who thinks they can stand in the way of our need to be free, to manage our own government, to be a force for good in the world, to protect our children and our land? Who thinks we are not willing to sweep away before us any who try to turn our sacred institutions of civic freedom to their greedy purposes?

On the road so far, I have seen a great nation. I have felt it hugging my shoulders, shaking my hand, cheering from across the way. I am so in love with it. I know you are too. Thank you, all.

Remarks the same day to Reform members who had split off:

As you begin this convention and these next critical years of American political reform, let someone who has fought many battles and won most of them eventually give you two bits of advice.

The first is obvious: If your cause is righteous, never give it up and you shall never be defeated. Keep at it. Hold the truth up before you and its power will never fail you. Defeat is reserved for those who give up. Even our death does not stop the stubborn advance of the truth, once we have put it in motion.

Now, never giving up may be the secret to victory, but how does one find the energy and the force of will to never give up? The key to that endurance is to be happy in warfare. Let me explain.

Politics today is characterized by anger and even hatred. If you have true enemies in politics, pray that their lives might be filled with anger and hatred, for no one so filled can ever win for very long. Anger drains your energy and makes you incapable of creative leadership. If you win, it will be short-lived. Ask the failed leaders of the so-called Republican Revolution if I am right. Negativity is negativity, and it has no place at the helm of a democracy. It doesn't know what to do when it gets to power.

Only joy and optimism—and love—can win in the long term. General Eisenhower said, "Pessimism never won any battle" He was right. Pessimism visualizes defeat. What we visualize, we help bring forth.

Now, I have told you that you must not give up, which is easy to say. And I have said that endurance is the product of optimism, which is also easy to say. How does one stay optimistic and full of love in a time such as ours?

You must keep this in mind. Life anywhere is a great adventure. But life in America is very special: America is a great—and, let me tell you, large—laboratory of the soul. We are a restless people, moving about, destroying our lives and starting over again, living several lifetimes in the space of one, while people in other reaches of the globe live comfortable or miserable half-lives by comparison. We are a mess, a disaster, a social wreck, but we are alive and learning and experimenting with life in a way that is quite new to the world and quite expanding to the soul, which is the very goal of life. The rest of the world knows this about America, and many of them wish they were here to joyfully suffer with us.

To know that we are the lucky participants in this privileged experiment ought to give us, whether friends or opponents, a secret camaraderie, a secret wink and smile across the battle lines, through the smoke and danger of our battles. In our political wars, let us keep our tongues therefore a little in our cheeks, understanding that the other fellow is not a villain, really, but just someone responsible for the defense of a different hill. We are a rich nation and can afford to be generous of spirit in the conduct of our politics—even where our battles involve life and death matters.

Take it as a fact, please, that anger in your heart is a signal from your brain that something or someone is not understood. The Stone Age reaction might be to get rid of that confusing thing, or strike out at it, but if we are civilized, we might instead try harder, and harder still, to study the thing and understand the thing until our anger turns to understanding. From that place, one can see the creative path to victory. This work is hard work. It is what goes on in a good university. It is what goes on in a good mind. It is the essential work of a creative leader.

I don't mean to suggest we should put away our swords and declare a picnic. There is certainly a difference between good and evil, which are real forces. **The force of good is, like gravity and like magnetism, a force that brings people together. The force of evil, like the force of explosive bombs or suburban sprawl or ethnic cleansing, is that which separates people and sets them against each other, makes them intolerant and, finally, demagogic or sociopathic or both. We need to be clear about the real nature of good and evil, and we must act with swift instinct to promote and save the good, and to repress and weed-out the evil in our political life. But we must not see people as evil, even if they are evil's captive agents for a time.** We need to save them from that captivity as best we can, within the limits of courtesy and democracy.

So, yes, we take on our great political fights and we do so with the great smile that shines from the very soul of truth. Love, one might say, is our secret strategy and motive. Why else would we want to change the world, if not for love? We must remind ourselves of this because this joy, this optimism, is the key to energy, endurance, persistence and victory. We need that secret key because we are at the dawn of our greatest battle yet in our long effort to advance America's freedoms and preserve its democracy. We had better be of right mind as we enter battle. If we enter with bitterness, or with pessimism, or with anger and hatred, we will not have the nearly superhuman strength we now need.

So, I advise you, this week, every week, elevate the debate, respect the opponent, and always assume honorable motives on the other side, even against all evidence. It is hard to do so. I slip into name-calling many times myself in the heat of rhetoric. It is draining and bad form, and it harms our own cause. If one intends to win, one is cheerful and generous. Good humor and generosity of spirit are the flags of unbeatable armies.

I said that we are facing a great battle. It is a battle of mythic proportion. It is this: America is losing its middle class, which is the foundation of its democracy. It is no surprise that the war chests of presidential candidates are exploding with cash this year: that is a simple reflection of the new concentration of wealth at one end of our population, and a reflection of the intent of the privileged class to preserve its position of advantage. Drive through this city and mark the doors of the families who can afford to give $1,000 to a presidential candidate and a senator and other officials, so that the family's needs might be served. For all the unmarked doors, we do not have a democracy, but an emergency—a crisis that deeply threatens our future as a free people.

My effort is to get big money out of our elections, and I believe that the McCain-Feingold soft money ban will be a good start—but only a start. In the long run our politics must again be the speeches at the Fourth of July picnic again, and the moneychangers must be swept out of the temples of democracy. It's time to get money out of the room so that we can be equal citizens once again, and that means dramatic changes to the way we communicate—freely communicate—political information in our society.

Once we return control of our politics to individual people, I think it will be possible to restore the vitality of the middle class. Right now, our local economies, our family businesses, our family time and family savings and family farms, our civic time, our public spaces, are being destroyed. The reins to all that are political reins, and we have to grab them back by forcing money out of our politics.

There are no villains in our midst not of our own making. We have been making them, building them up for a century now, and they are getting too big to handle.

At the beginning of this century, Theodore Roosevelt, that great Republican, worried that businesses were getting out-scaled, and that the family farmer and the family business would be crushed by the great corporations then forming. He instituted anti-trust laws and he pushed corporations out of politics with strong laws that protected us until some holes were punched in these walls during the past twenty years.

Like a frontier family threatened by a shutter blown open in a blizzard, we must struggle to get that opening closed again before our democracy dies in a blizzard of money of selfish intent.

Where are we at this present moment in the history of America? I will tell you what I find as I walk across it. I find communities separated by income, where there is no sense of true community. I find families splintered by the demands of careers, because the companies they work for have no regard for the time and pay it takes to be a proper family, the resources it takes, or the geographic stability it takes. You may argue all day long about whether or not it takes a village to raise a child, but I will tell you that it at least takes a family, and by that, I mean grandparents and great-grandparents and uncles and cousins and family friends. The brutal disruption of families by corporations, and by families that put the dollar chase above the other needs of their family members, means that children are growing up almost as street children. They are angry and alone, and they are being pushed to antisocial tendencies. They need their families. The great experiment of this century, the experiment that you can scatter families to the wind, that you can scatter communities out

into the fields, that you can scatter races and income groups into enclaves of their own, is an expensive disaster. And yet, there are great industries profiting from our misery and dedicated to our continued strife.

There is only one way out for us, and it is a long shot. Walking across America I have seen a people too busy, too stressed in their everyday lives to be members of a community. If parents are thus antisocial, pulled and pushed as they are by the demands of a wholly commercial culture, is it any surprise that their children will be antisocial too, or that they will join supremacist cults and do violence? It is hardly surprising at all. It is how they have been shown to live by parents who have no time for their communities, their neighbors, their own family members.

I have seen retired people so caught up in their hobbies and motorhomes that they have no time for their families, their communities or their country. They think they have paid their dues and can relax. Well, no, that is what heaven is for. We all have work to do while we are alive, and, if we do not do it, people suffer. Things don't get done. Children don't get cared for. Single mothers don't get help. The hungry don't get fed. And, all the while, doing these right things is more fulfilling than anything else that can be done in this life.

So, yes, be the conservatives you are, but work to conserve what our democracy needs to survive and prosper. And in your political fights with others, even those in your own party, act with great courtesy and respect for the other person's views. Only that will give you the joy to keep going; and winning is about keeping going. Thank you.

Together at the Table of Power

Little Rock First Baptist Church, Sunday, August 22, 1999. Salon Magazine: "When Doris Haddock finishes a speech, you find yourself wishing she'd run for president, or something. True, at age 89 she's off to a rather late start. In Little Rock, Haddock spoke at Central High School, site of the 1957 integration crisis, as well as in a church pulpit where Dr. Martin Luther King Jr. preached in the 1960s. The congregation initially eyed Haddock with some skepticism, but by the time she was finished speaking, they were cheering and surrounding her."

Dear friends, it is a great honor to stand here in your midst, to stand here speaking where Dr. Martin Luther King, Jr. once stood and spoke. Here was a man—and we feel his presence in this place—who came into this world to speak the truth. Some people listened and understood, and some did not.

And the truth was this and remains this: that we are brothers and sisters; that our struggles to overcome injustice and unfairness, cruelty and oppression are only successful in the long run where our method is love—love of one another, love of our enemies.

When we hate our enemies, we stop praying for them. And when we stop praying for them, how can we ever hope to turn them around?

We all have known family members who were on the wrong path and who created turmoil and pain in our families. We pray for them, in love, in the hope of turning them around. Well, America is a family, too. And our struggles are family struggles, where love is the greatest power and, in the long run of history, the only enduring power. Look at the best things—the lasting things—that America has done for itself and for the world in the centuries of our history: they are changes motivated by love, by a dream of equality, by a dream of peace and justice. The changes wrought by hatred fall away, while the changes wrought by love endure.

The use of love and truth to bring forth justice nonviolently was brought to this nation by Dr. King, and we thank him for it. He studied it and learned it from the writings of Mr. Gandhi. Mr. Gandhi learned it from the writings of John Ruskin and Leo Tolstoy, who learned it from American nonviolent abolitionists Frederick Douglass and William Lloyd Garrison, who learned about it from the Sermon on the Mount.

Thus, the great need for justice and freedom in America,

the need to end slavery, resulted in a ripple of thought that spread and grew across the world, and came back to us in our time of need, thanks to Dr. King. He brought that teaching here, to this place, this room. Such is the enduring power of the Sermon on the Mount and of love itself in the world.

Nonviolent political action is, according to the instructions of Gandhi and the practices of Dr. King, a five-fold technique that we must always remember. It should be taught in our schools. It should be remembered wherever people gather with the intention of improving their communities or their world. Here are the five steps:

Number One: Determine the truth of a situation before taking a strong position. If it is an injustice, can it be clearly documented? Bring in the experts if you can. Be sure what you are advocating is actually and demonstrably the truth.

Number Two: Communicate your findings, your position and your request for change in a respectful and achievable way to the people who have the direct power to correct the situation. Don't ask someone for something they don't have the power to give. Don't shout on the sidewalks if you have not yet communicated respectfully with the parties in authority and have respectfully waited for a reply.

Number Three: If the response does not come, or is insufficient, bring public attention to the issue. Work openly so the thinking process of the entire community can be engaged. Gandhi and King were accused of staging events for the media. Of course they did. Social change is a public process, and it does not happen for the good when it happens in the dark. Engage the community openly so that they can be a part of the debate and the decision. This consciousness-raising works easiest in a democracy, but few governments, no matter how authoritarian, are wholly immune from public sentiment.

Number Four: If those in authority will not correct a very serious situation that must be resolved, despite an open airing of the issue, then the advocates must be willing to make sacrifices to demonstrate the seriousness of the matter. When King marched forward toward baton-swinging policemen in Selma, he showed that the issue was important. When Gandhi led marches and gave speeches that he knew would lead to his imprisonment that day, and when his followers stood in long lines to be clubbed by security forces standing in the way of their rightful path, the world stopped its daily routine to inquire about the injustice that motivated the self-sacrifice of these people and what, in fairness, should be done. And here is the difficult key to success: It is in the endless willingness of the advocates to make a continuing sacrifice that guarantees their victory. Few injustices are powerful enough, or have enough supporters, to stand against the flow of such generosity.

"You have been the veterans of creative suffering," Dr. King told his followers in the "I Have a Dream" speech. Well, creative suffering is something we all have the power to do. Along with aggressive and creative moral leadership, it is one of the

most powerful forces for change in the world. It is always in our pocket, ready for the call of our conscience.

There is a fifth step, made necessary by the fact that the non-violence technique, when properly practiced, nearly always wins. The fifth step, as developed by Mr. Gandhi and as practiced by Dr. King, is to be gracious in victory—to remember that your enemy is your brother, and that you should therefore settle the dispute kindly, accepting some compromises and granting as much face-saving courtesy as possible to the other side. You will meet again, after all, and why not as friends? Gandhi said on many occasions that we have to love and respect our adversaries because they are our brothers and sisters, and also that they are parts of ourselves and of our God. He meant it.

Here is a passage from his autobiography:

"Man and his deed are two distinct things. It is quite proper to resist and attack a system, but to resist and attack its author is tantamount to resisting and attacking oneself. For we are all tarred with the same brush, and are children of one and the same Creator, and as such the divine powers within us are infinite. To slight a single human being is to slight those divine powers, and thus to harm not only that being, but with him the whole world."

Dr. King believed much the same, and you can hear it clearly in the "I Have a Dream" speech, where he calls us together as "all of God's children."

These are the five steps that gave India its freedom and which gave America its second revolution of independence at a moment when it could have devolved into a full race war. In the moment when King left this world, the violence that could have been ours all along showed itself in Watts and Detroit and a hundred other cities and towns. There is no courage in a thrown bottle of gasoline, especially where an innocent person is harmed, or a family's life work is burned to the ground. True courage is what we saw in the buses arriving at Little Rock's Central High School and in the Selma march. Sometimes, irrepressible anger moves politics toward justice, but the truer and surer course is given to us in the Great Sermon: Love works. Love wins. Love endures. It is the foundation of our religion, and it must be of our politics.

In my walk across the country, I speak against the idea that those individuals and those corporations with the greatest wealth should be able to buy our elections and our candidates and our representatives, diverting their attention from the needs of the people, and preventing honest candidates from winning.

That we have a problem, that money has become more important than ideas in our political debate, is a proven fact. That this huge, national influence-peddling scheme results in a mass diversion of the public wealth from where it is needed to where privileged people would have it for their own use, is no longer a debatable point. When I walk with this message, I have the advantage of speaking the simple truth, proven by every major research institution, on both the right and left of political life, who have taken the time to investigate the issue.

We have asked those in power to remedy the situation, and they have refused. We have asked them again, and again they have refused.

We have engaged the press of the nation to shine a great light on this cancer, and still there is no movement by the leaders. Transparency is no cure for the metastasized cancer of political corruption.

And so, step four: we must reveal the depth of our concern. We must make a sacrifice of ourselves to demonstrate the serious nature of this problem, and this injustice. All great political change requires pain. Mr. Gandhi and Dr. King advised us to take that pain upon ourselves, not to inflict it upon others. And that is what we must do: sacrifice and stand more and more forcefully in the way of this injustice. If we fail, it will because we did not sacrifice sufficiently. We showed up only on Saturdays when it was convenient for us, even though Congress was out of town. We made speeches to ourselves about ourselves instead of into the hearts of our countrymen about their own freedoms and futures. The side that wins in politics is the one with the greater empathy, even if it does not look like empathy—call it the greater connection to the great mass of our people.

The message we must convey is simple: that there is no true equality in America so long as only the rich are represented at the table of power. That is not democracy. There can be no true justice in America so long as only the privileged make the rules and build the jails for those outside the rooms of power. That is not democracy.

Only when we all sit together at the table of power can we do the right things by our communities.

We need quality preschools, affordable or free, for all our young families. We will not get them if we are not all at the table of power.

We all need affordable health care. We will not get it if we are not all at the table of power.

We need quality public schools that will inspire and raise up our children to their highest potential, not suppress them and lead them to despair and trouble. We will not get such schools if we are not all at the table of power.

We need programs so that dropout rates evaporate to nothing and so that every child has a positive vision of his or her future in this nation. We will not get those programs if we are not all at the table of power.

We need to make a college education as affordable as a high school education, because those who do not go on are doomed to poverty in the economy of the coming century. Moving from high school to college should be as automatic as moving from grade school to high school, and it is in the clear national interest of America to make it so. But it will not happen if we are not all at the table of power.

We need to make sure that the rising wealth of America is felt first, not last, in its poorest communities, with a new wealth of personal opportunities so that parents can provide for their children and have time left over to raise their children—and so that children can see a happy future. This will not happen if we are not all at the table of power.

In this new era of electronic communication and commerce, we must include all our children and all our families. We are divided enough already, and we don't need a digital divide to further separate us. We need to provide connection to all our people. This will not happen if we are not all at the table of power.

We need employment and training programs to provide real access to all groups, all races, all people, to every rank of every career. We need to turn renters into homeowners and open up the capital markets that enable family businesses to start and grow.

We can insist on such changes when we all sit together at the table of power. If we are separated, we are not equal.

This is an agenda of love. For, when we are in the same room, looking eye-to-eye and speaking heart-to-heart, it is hard for us to deny each other justice and equality as Americans. If I tell you what my children need that I cannot provide, you will help me provide for them. If you tell me what your children need that you cannot provide, I will help you provide for them. That is the essence of self-government in a free land. The trick is to get us all in the room, all at the table, and campaign finance reform is one of the keys to making that finally happen.

We do have the ability to publicly finance our elections, to make them as free as the candidates' speeches at a Fourth of July picnic. And we must do it. We own the airwaves, after all. The billions of dollars we save by eliminating the corporate welfare that flows from today's corrupt campaign system could fund the public financing of elections, with nearly $50 billion left over each year. How we could better take care of our children with that!

We are a free and equal people—in theory and in law. But I don't believe we will have real equality, practical equality, and I don't believe we will have democracy—practical democracy—until the influence of billionaire money is reduced in the elective process and people can run on the strength of their character and ideas. To take money from those you regulate was bribery a thousand years ago, and it is bribery today. And while our leaders take campaign bribes with one hand—bribes that deprive us of our democracy—with the other hand they falsely pledge allegiance to the great dream of America—the dream so many have died for.

"They promise them freedom, but they themselves are slaves of corruption; for whatever overcomes a man, to that he is enslaved." (Second Book of Peter, Chapter 2, verse 19).

And from Psalm 26:

"Gather not my soul with sinners, nor my life with bloody men, in whose hands is mischief, and their right hand is full of bribes. But as for me, I will walk in mine integrity: redeem me, and be merciful unto me. My foot standeth in an even place: in the congregations will I bless the Lord."

I bless the Lord in this congregation and thank Him for bringing me safely to this place. I thank you for the honor of being able to address you here, under the Lord's roof and in the presence of Dr. King's spirit. I pray for those in this country who have the burden of responsibility for leading us. I pray that they shake off the chains of unrighteous obligation that tighten around them through the present campaign finance system. I pray that they will have the courage to do the right thing for themselves and for their fellow Americans. I know they are not happy with the present situation, nor are we, the people.

I hope the campaign finance reform movement and the civil rights movement can join hands. Either the common people will rule this land, or they will be ruled. Either justice and loving mercy will be the condition of our communities, or the present harsh regime will continue to erode our lives and foment conflict and alienation within our communities.

We are walking together on the high road of history. We are on even ground, now, because so many sacrifices have been made behind us. We have nothing to lose that we care about, and our shared freedom to gain. We are walking in love, our successes sparkling behind us, and we cannot be stopped so long as our souls are alive, and our souls live forever.

Thank you. Please join me in Memphis on September 7th if you can, to keep walking where Dr. King fell, and then on to Washington through the winter.

To the Apologists of Corruption

> *Ms. Haddock's remarks from the balcony of the Lorraine Motel to a large crowd in Memphis on September 7, 1999 — the first of two speeches she made from that historic balcony (the other was in 2004). She walked to the site with Dick Gregory and members of the sanitation union who walked with King on his last day.*

We are on hallowed ground. The petty affairs of the day fade away at this place, where the courage and pain of a righteous life suddenly transcended to the eternal. And with that transcendence, the light from above that shows us the way to justice and love became, for all time, one soul brighter. Did King die here? The part of him we love, his soul, will never die. And so, his voice still rings in our ears and he still implores us to make brotherhood, love and self-sacrifice our own tools for change. We hear you, Dr. King.

In this place, it is easy to remember that our brothers and sisters of every color have sacrificed their lives to advance our shared dream of a land of equality and plenty. We have not made these sacrifices in order to separate our people into rich and poor, privileged and oppressed. Dr. King was in this very place because he believed that equal economic opportunity is the partner of political equality.

Our people are more economically divided now than they were when King walked this way. The tax and labor and business laws of this nation drive that division, and those policies are held hostage by a corrupt Congress and its system of campaign finance bribery and billion-dollar political favors. These favors are paid at the expense of programs that could make our society fairer and less troubled.

Whole parts of our society, stripped of other opportunities, have fallen into illegal markets to survive. A young generation of urban poor is in jail or in the justice system. Our families are working too many jobs and too many hours to be able to raise their families properly.

It is the duty of leaders to shape society so that the great masses of its people can work to provide decently for their families and their futures. Our leaders, distracted by the corruption of the campaign finance system, are failing that duty.

They pass laws that destroy the jobs and lower the protections for workers, that segregate the people into rich communities and communities of despair, that provide jails instead of education, shelters instead of decent housing, and toxic pollution instead of healthy environments for our children. They do it to favor the wealthy elite who underwrite campaigns to keep them in power.

We must replace this bribery with the full public financing of our elections, so that candidates may speak as freely to the community as they did in the days when public ally-funded candidate debates in the park sufficed. We must get big money out of politics before it destroys us utterly.

Americans are disheartened, but we reformers must not despair. We must help bring forward the day when ordinary people can speak as equals at the table of power to decide the affairs of our government.

Our democracy is sacred ground. It is red with the sacrifices of our people. We are here today to honor those sacrifices, not with our words, but with our deeds.

To the apologists of corruption in Congress, like Mr. McConnell of Kentucky, understand, sir, that, just like those who stood atop the school steps to block the historic arrival of desegregation, you cannot stand forever atop the Capitol steps, your arms folded against the American people's longing for a democracy worthy of our national sacrifices.

I thank Mr. Dick Gregory and the Memphis sanitation workers who have walked with me today. I hope you will walk with me again in January in Washington. By then I might need a hand up the Capitol steps, and I hope that we, as American brothers and sisters, might go into that great temple of freedom together, with Dr. King beside us and in our hearts. Thank you.

33

Your Answer, Mr. McConnell

On Saturday, November 6, 1999, Ms. Haddock walked into Louisville and assembled a rally of 160 people outside the office of Kentucky's U.S. Senator Mitch McConnell—the principal opponent of campaign finance reform in Congress. As with most of her speeches, it was widely covered by local newspapers, radio and three television stations. This particular speech was run in its entirety in the newspaper, with a favorable editorial comment. People Magazine also covered the event. Senator McConnell's effort to stall the issuance of an event permit was discovered and defeated, allowing the event to take place legally. "We would have done it anyway," Ms. Haddock told a reporter, "the Constitution is our permit."

Thank you for this welcome. I have so enjoyed walking through Kentucky—the beauty is overwhelming. This is a wonderful state, filled with great people. Today, I want to speak about one great Kentuckian in particular, and that is Senator Mitch McConnell, whose office I have come to after 2,400 miles of walking.

He is on the other side of the battle lines in our effort to return American democracy to the human scale—our effort to get the $100,000 check out of politics. But he is a most worthy opponent.

He fiercely represents his beliefs and the interests of Kentucky in Washington.

He sits as chairman of the Senate Rules Committee, which has jurisdiction over federal election laws and the administration of the Senate. He is the chairman of the Foreign Operations Subcommittee, a key foreign policy committee, and is a member of the Agriculture and Appropriations committees. These positions of leadership indicate that he is held in high esteem by his fellow Senators. He is also the chairman of the National Republican Senatorial Committee, which means he is responsible for supporting the campaigns of Republican Senate candidates in every state. In 1997, he raised millions for these campaigns from corporations and from wealthy contributors. He is raising more for the upcoming election.

When he speaks on the Senate floor, his arguments are well reasoned and a delight to listen to. They make good reading, like the orations of Cicero of ancient Rome. He defends our Constitution—as he sees our Constitution—with a vengeance.

You are waiting for me to say something unkind.

In fact, I have come here to do him a favor, and to ask a favor. I will scold a bit, but I am not here to vilify him.

He asked a question on the Senate floor recently and got no answer. I have, on foot, brought him his answer today.

In the recent campaign finance reform debate in the Senate, he rather sharply attacked Senator McCain, when Mr. McCain had the audacity to suggest that the hundreds of millions of dollars being spent by special interests to influence the passage of laws in Congress might indeed be influencing the passage of laws in Congress. Mr. McConnell thought that was an outrageous assumption and asked for the names of any Members of Congress so low as to bend their votes toward the interests of contributors, like flowers toward the sun. Specifically, he said this:

"I ask the Senator from Arizona; how can it be corruption if no one is corrupt? That is like saying the gang is corrupt but none of the gangsters are. If there is corruption, someone must be corrupt."

He also said: "It is astonishing. We have here rampant charges of corruption and yet no names are named..."

Mr. McConnell demanded the names of those who were corrupt. Mr. McCain, for reasons of friendship, courtesy and the dignity of the Senate—such as it is—did not name names.

But Mr. McConnell persisted, demanding that Senator McCain give a name. Mr. McConnell was like a reverse-Diogenes, searching the dark corners of the Senate chamber with his lantern for one dishonest man.

I have come here today to answer the question asked by Mr. McConnell, and to end his long search.

Lately, Mr. McCain has been accused of having a temper. But he did not answer Mr. McConnell's question in anger on the Senate floor.

Nor will I answer it in anger here, though it is true I can get a little testy, too. My feet do hurt sometimes and need to be taped so that I can walk. I wear a steel corset to help my back, and it can sometimes make my words a little sharp toward the end of the day. Torture, even a little of it, does make you testy.

I have come a long way to address great men like Senator McConnell and tell them what Americans are saying about the condition of our democracy, and the role of big money in that democracy. The road wears on me sometimes and I am tempted to say in anger what all America seems to know except a few sheltered men and women whom we care for in a special room in Washington and who do not seem to notice deterioration when it comes over them slowly, or corruption when it becomes the water they swim in.

The answer to your question, Senator McConnell, is elementary.

You ask, "how can it be corruption if no one is corrupt? If there is corruption, someone must be corrupt." You are right, of course. Your analysis is pure genius. Someone must be corrupt. Who can it be?

Perhaps it is the bagman who shakes down American industries in return for protection in Congress and for special tax breaks from the party in power, while average, working Americans struggle mightily to make ends meet. Have you seen such a person, Senator McConnell?

In 1997, Senator McConnell, when you took $791,945 from insurance interests who needed protection from patient rights efforts, and $602,885 from oil and gas interests who needed a free flow of tax benefits and protections against pollution laws, and $597,915 from communications interests who wanted free access to the digital spectrum and a free hand to merge into giant monopolies, you might have seen such a bag man in their offices. He's the man you were asking about on the Senate floor.

When you let a Ukraine group host a fundraiser for you in 1996, and you used your position as Chairman of the Appropriations Committee to provide a $225 million appropriation for development programs in Ukraine, did you see another fellow there, trading money for public policy? That's the fellow. He is at such meetings and making such deals almost daily, year in and out.

More to the point, Senator McConnell, though I admire your abilities and your achievements, and the hard work you perform for this state and for all of us, you are the man you asked Senator McCain about. And you are not alone.

The House and the Senate are full of some of the best minds and most caring hearts in America, and they are being ethically destroyed by the financial demands of campaigning in the modern age…

A Brisk Walk Across the Country

Remarks in Clarksburg, West Virginia, January 1, 2000, completing one year on the road, after climbing the Appalachian Range in blizzard conditions:

Some people do wonder if I have taken my activism a little too far. They ask me what on Earth I am doing, walking across the country at my age. I can tell you I am not doing it for my health—though it has done me no harm, and perhaps a brisk walk across the country is something every American should do… there is no better way to fall in love with this land and its people—they are so kind and bright and interesting, and so dedicated to the aspirational dreams of America.

In my long walk I have indeed seen quite a bit. I have crossed the Mojave Desert that I thought would never end—its dust and sand swirling around me. I have landed in a hospital and a rodeo—my first—and in more than a few parades. I have slept in the modest homes of Native Americans in the Arizona desert and walked with children and senators, mayors and vagabonds. I have met elderly women who have pressed their precious food into my hands, though they themselves must eat pet food to stretch their budgets. I have cried with them when we parted. I have watched Texas cowboys and cowgirls break horses in the cool dusk under Texas stars. I have cut my way through weeds and waded across rivers. I have walked with the great leaders of the American Civil Rights movement through the South, and even found myself preaching government reform from a pulpit where Dr. King once preached. I have stood and made speeches here and there, on the steps of senator's offices and in the tiny meeting rooms of so many little communities along the way.

I have met and walked with so many wonderful people of every race, age, income and political persuasion. But through it all, I have yet to meet one person who believes we should hand over our democracy to those who would use their big dollars to take it from us. I have yet to talk with the one man or woman or child who wants their senator to be beholden to the special interest check writers who step in line in front of us all, stealing our representation. As a nation, I tell you we are of one mind on the matter of special interest, big money politics: We are through with it.

Our Town

January 3, 2000, Clarksburg, West Virginia:

Thank you. It is a great pleasure to be here. Clarksburg is a beautiful community, and I know how you love it. Your people have been here for centuries, surviving deep snows and wide floods, and you have watched your children grow and your friends grow old. You, yourself, are still looking fine, however.

I know about the magic of being from a good town and loving it.

There is a stage play that I'm sure you know, entitled "Our Town," by Mr. Thornton Wilder. It is about life and death in a small New Hampshire town. More exactly, it is about all the beauty we can miss if we are not fully awake to the brief magic of life. Mr. Wilder wrote the play while residing in the community where I live. Ages ago, I got to play the lead role of Our Town when the play was new and so was I. We of the region take his play as a correct description of the heartbreaking beauty of life in a caring community of decent people. The area is called Dublin and Peterborough and Keene, New Hampshire, just west of Manchester and along the skirt of Mount Monadnock.

Now, Mr. Wilder was careful not to start any arguments about where the real Our Town might be, and whether some of the characters might therefore have real counterparts. In the very beginning of the play, he therefore cites the longitude and latitude of the town. If you go to a map, however, you will see that the coordinates he gives describe the middle of Massachusetts Bay, quite a way out in the water. So, respecting his wishes, we do not claim to be the true Our Town. We do, however, live and die as he described, and we understand the emotions that stirred within him as he wrote.

He wrote in an area of 32 little cabins set up for writers and artists by Edward and Marian MacDowell. At the MacDowell Colony, Mr. Wilder wrote his play, and America's great music composer, Aaron Copeland, wrote much of his masterwork, Appalachian Spring. Virgil Thomson wrote Mother of Us All. Leonard Bernstein completed his great symphonic Mass.

Over 4,000 artists and writers have taken their turn working in that beautiful and harmonious setting, including Edwin Arlington Robinson, Milton Avery, James Baldwin, Willa Cather, Jules Feiffer, Studs Terkel, Alice Walker and many, many others.

I spent most of my weekends for a half century at another such colony, called Dundee, several hours up the mountain, where we spent our leisure hours with great thinkers and artists, and where we prepared our big meal together each evening, and put on plays for each other in the theater built for just us and our children.

This all may be something of a revelation to many people who have grown up in big cities or towns under clouds of oppression. They may not have imagined that humans can form happy and creative communities—that they can make something of a heaven for themselves here on Earth. It can be done. I have done it all my life, and I assume that many of you have, too.

For those not so fortunate—if they would like to find their way to a community of love and courtesy where the purpose of living is to reach one's full potential as a creative human being and help others do the same—I have some advice.

There is a secret to the creation and nurturing of true community. Once people know the secret, they can create community anywhere they choose—any place they happen to find themselves.

The secret is to take the world as your own—to take full responsibility for it. Once a person steps into the circle of those who take responsibility for the happy operation of the community, once someone decides that they are not a customer of government, but government itself, the magic of community begins, and, as long as we are breathing and thinking and our hearts are beating, the world is ours to shape according to our values.

There are many people who would like us to believe that the world is theirs, not ours, so that they might steal our world from us—steal our lives from us. They would like us to be their little slaves, mindlessly working for their happiness at the expense of our own and accepting all the evils of the world as somehow necessary. That is nonsense.

More and more, I am seeing homeless people along my walk. If a man or woman or child is on a street with no place to go, it is not only a great affront to their dignity and safety, but also to yours, though you are but driving by. That homeless person is a billboard statement to you from the financially powerful members of our economy, who indeed have the resources to shelter everyone in a decent home. The intended message is that you are at risk too, if you are too often late for work, if you are too troublesome with your demands for justice of any kind. The misery of others is thus used as a weapon against us all. It is a statement that says, "this is not your community; you do not have the power to impose your humanitarian and other values on this place." And so, our answer to that must be to help everyone and make safety nets of our own devising, so that no one will fear to live free and the community will be a true reflection of our values. It will be Our Town.

When some people accept the "them versus us" divide between the people and the government, they are buying into the lie that destroys democracy. They need to wake up, and, frankly, we need to wake each other up from that hypnosis from time to time.

The violence in our society is a symptom of that hypnosis. A real citizen, a person who takes responsibility for the community, is not someone who returns poison with poison, rudeness with rudeness, violence with violence—for to do so would be playing but a bit part in a minor play. When someone can return rudeness with concern, poison with understanding, violence with peace, they are not being ruled by others. They are free. The world is theirs, and it begins to turn their way, toward their higher values, because they are not giving rudeness what it needs to survive, nor violence what it needs to grow. They are spreading their consciousness over the larger view and taking responsibility for the workings of their community.

In our land, the rise of violence is held as a mystery. It is no mystery to me. It is what happens when people, young and old, no longer feel responsible for their communities. There is a great, and now global, corporate-political complex at work to strip people of their ability to feel responsible for their communities, of their ability to feel connected with its needs and valuable to its operation.

In my long walk, I am trying to get some new laws passed that will make it easier, I hope, for people to be responsible for their own communities and their own government. I worry that the influence of very rich companies and very rich people make it difficult for regular people to feel that they are in charge of their own affairs. We need to get the big, $100,000 special interest contributions out of our elections. Those contributions shout down you and me, and there is no true free speech nor true political equality so long as this condition persists.

I would not be on this path if I did not believe that America is my responsibility; I am responsible for its workings, as are you.

Even in the very act of trying to help, I find my happiness and I find a creative community of people. In this way, we have already won. We always win if we will only wake ourselves from the hypnosis some would impose on us and take responsibility as the happy leaders of our communities, our land and our Earth.

In this generation, the fate of our natural environment, and of our democratic environment will be decided. Only great leadership, and great love, can get us through the times ahead. We must all take our parts in this great drama. It is more than politics; it is a struggle of the soul, and it is exquisitely personal to each of us.

I have talked long enough for someone who is supposed to be out walking. But let me say that I take my town with me. Our Town always travels with each of us. The longitude and latitude of it cross upon our hearts. We bring the good community into being with our love and our relentless consciousness. We mustn't fail to appreciate the magical moment of life, and to fully participate in it joyfully and constructively, never giving an inch to injustice, unfairness or inequality, nor ever forgetting the long line of people we have known and loved in the great  circle that extends well beyond the world we know.

Thank you for listening to me today and thank you for your very warm hospitality along a cold and snowy road.

The Efficacy of Sacrifice

January 8, 2000, at West Virginia University in Morgantown:

Thank you for being here to welcome me. It is an honor to be here with you in Morgantown. It may seem odd to you that an 89-year-old woman—almost 90—should walk across the country for an issue like campaign finance reform. It sounds like something CPAs should worry about, not old folks from New Hampshire.

Nevertheless, on January 1st of last year, I began my walk in Los Angeles and I have been walking ever since, usually ten miles a day. It has been a great adventure.

That you might better understand how this kind of protest works, let me describe what has happened to me again and again on my walk. When I got across the Mojave Desert in California, I found myself at the Arizona town of Parker, on the Colorado River. The mayor of that lively town is a wonderful woman named Sandy Pierce. Now, I don't know if Sandy cared too much about campaign finance reform before I got there, though she well may have. But after we met—and after people congratulated me for crossing that big desert where many others have died, and after Good Morning America and National Public Radio interviewed me—people were very curious about campaign finance reform. Sandy understood immediately what I was talking about. Within a few hours, she was introducing me all over town with a little speech like this: "Now I would like you to meet Doris Haddock. She has just walked here from Los Angeles, through the Mojave." People's eyes would open a little wider. She would continue: "She is doing it to publicize the need for campaign finance reform. She is upset that big money interests are calling the shots in our elections, and we no longer have much of a say. She thinks that is a huge problem for us all. She says that all the people who have died in wars to defend our democracy would want us to defend it now, from those who are buying it from under us."

Well, all I would have to do after that was smile and shake hands. People would immediately see that what I was doing did, in fact, relate to serious issues that disturbed them, too.

Then, of course, the local newspaper reporter would want to know about campaign finance reform. If someone would walk so far across that desert for it, it must be important. And so, I would explain how there are laws limiting what a person can give to any one candidate, and that these laws are meant to preserve the health of the democratic system. I would explain that there is a soft money loophole that gets around those laws. The loophole allows corporations, unions or wealthy individuals to give unlimited amounts of money to parties. The parties can pass those dollars along to candidates. What is the point of contribution limits, if you can just use this back door?

Well, reporters are quick studies by trade. So, wherever I have gone, reporters have quickly learned about the issue and written about it. Large newspapers have looked anew at the issue, and some have changed their positions, including big papers like the Dallas Morning News, now demanding campaign finance reform. Now, could I have done as well if I sat back in New Hampshire and wrote letters to the editor? Probably not. People respect serious and sincere sacrifice, and they will listen to you on account of it.

Having newspaper reporters and editors who understand and care about campaign finance reform is very bad news, indeed, for anti-reform Members of Congress who were later interviewed by those same news people.

Now, back to campaign reform for a moment. Some of your friends may ask, why shouldn't they be able to spend as much money as they want on a candidate? It is a free country, and that is a part of free speech, isn't it? Well, tell them this: If money is speech, how can we be equal citizens? If money is speech and we are all in the same room, trying to run a democracy, then some of us are mute and some richest of us have bullhorns. It is reasonable to put some limits on the money going into campaigns, if only to make it so that all can be fairly heard.

As you know, big corporate money has taken up residence in Washington in a very serious way and has now taken over the process. If you decide, as a free citizen of America, that you believe we need to do a better job of reducing greenhouse gasses, or of protecting natural resources, or any other cause you believe in, and you go to Washington to press your case, I ask you: will you be talking to those Senators and Representatives, and will they be listening to your arguments and making decisions based on the best facts and the best interests of our country and our world? Today, they will not, and that is the tragic condition we must not allow to persist. They are all running on high-speed treadmills of fundraising that only give them time to listen to big money lobbyists, and then to do their bidding. They rationalize it, of course, thinking that, in the big picture of things, they are doing the best for America. They are lying to themselves, and to all of us.

K Street, where the biggest corporate lobbyists have their

offices in Washington, is the main feeding trough for this piggery. The big lobbyists put money out in the troughs each morning on K Street, and then the great oinking starts up on Capitol Hill. Soon, members of Congress are all nudging each other at the troughs. It's enough to make you a vegetarian.

I am walking to Washington, but I am not going first to the Capitol building, as that is only the puppet theater these days. I am walking first to K Street, the true center of power, where we will show Washington to itself for the shameful place it has become.

Enough negativity. Let me tell you that, for every negative thought I have had along this long walk, there have been a thousand beautiful moments. Americans are truly kind, interesting, odd, beautiful and smart people. I recommend that, someday, when it is not escapism, you don a backpack and go see it all for yourself. I don't think you should wait until you are 90. I expect that most of you younger people will live 150 years or more, so you might think about doing it twice: once through the north, and once through the south. And leave time for the rest of the world, too.

On your walks, you will see how important political leadership is in the lives of the people. When we do not have leaders that care about fairness, and health, and the fulfillment of the educational potential of each person, what we get is what we have gotten: poverty, illiteracy, dysfunctional communities, a disappearing middle class, widespread emotional depression and political anger. I am not saying that it is the government's role to run our lives; I am saying we are the government, and we run this country for our mutual benefit, unless powerful interests get in our way, stealing our common resources and our very lives.

When that happens, we must act, and that is what I am doing for myself, and what you must do for yourself. For this is your land. It is not someone else's. This is your life, not someone else's. Your freedoms and your position of responsibility as a member of a self-governing community have been paid for in blood by the people who came before you. You owe it to them, and most of all to yourselves, to sweep away anything that gets between you and your rightful place as the free member of a free community.

Up the road a way, near Cumberland, I will mark mile 3,000 and my 90th year. I am almost finished with this walk, but I am far from finished with this work. In Washington, we will make a determination regarding who in Congress is for reform, and who is too busy with their snouts in the sludge to make a commitment to reform. On the basis of that determination, I will be active in the states in the coming election year to try to defeat some Members of Congress who stand in the way of reform. We only need a few more votes in the Senate to achieve a good start.

So, this is serious and long-term work, but I am up for it, and I hope you are, too. Our democracy and the biological survival of our planet are in the balance. And aren't we fortunate to live in a time when so much is at stake—when each of us has such a fine challenge to our souls? Thank you all.

A Modest Proposal for Sacrifice

> *Ms. Haddock's remarks to friends and supporters via email on January 17, 2000, in remembrance of the birthday of Martin Luther King, Jr.:*

In my walk across America, I have met, in so many faces, the clear-eyed sense of fairness and equality that has guided our nation's slow but steady progress. This sense of fairness has a big, farmer's handshake and a direct preacher's voice. When you are in the presence of it—when it shouts a friendly hi across a road to you—why, you know you have not walked too far; you are still in the land of Jefferson and King, Whitman, Steinbeck, Susan B, and ever so fortunate you and me.

I met a gentleman in Arizona, Mr. Eddie Basha, a grocer of proud, Lebanese descent. In the early 1950s, Eddie was on a high

school football team in an Arizona farming town. A local restaurant owner promised the team a steak dinner if they would win the big game. They did, and the team showed up to claim their dinner. One of their team members was Black. The restaurant owner said he could not serve him. Eddie, knowing nothing yet of the simmering Civil Rights Movement, but knowing plenty about fairness, told the restaurant owner that he was being unfair. Eddie organized a boycott of the restaurant until the owner finally agreed to serve every one of every color. The other restaurants in town soon followed, not wanting to see those linebackers and eloquent Eddie on their sidewalk next.

To nurture that sense of fairness, and to bring it to life with acts of personal leadership, are what we must be about as parents and community leaders. As always, we must teach by example. Fairness and leadership are everything to the life of a democracy.

A simple sense of fairness is the great genius of America's enduring aspiration. That is what drives our equal rights movements and our politics, courts and councils. It used to drive our Congress, too—I remember that time, before big money bought it out from under us.

We will change it back, for we are good at fixing up this old democracy.

Raising the level of fairness in our society is always painful and often dangerous. Martin Luther King, Jr., as a student and teacher of nonviolent protest, followed the example and writings of Mr. Gandhi, who was himself instructed—indirectly through Ruskin and Tolstoy—by American Quakers. Dr. King brought this teaching back to our Nation at a dangerous time, when we most needed it. He told us we must take the pain of moral progress upon ourselves, rather than inflict it upon others—what an amazing and ethical concept! And more amazing still, is the fact that it works better than any other method of social change.

If we would be successful, we must suffer the batons, not wield them. We must suffer hunger and cold, not inflict them. The political and cultural changes which have come about through self-sacrifice tend to be good and lasting changes. Changes wrought by violence are often filled with unanticipated evils.

Dr. King looked out upon mid-Twentieth Century America and he did not have to look far to see that his enemy was massive, institutionalized unfairness—rooted so deeply that many could not see it or imagine the world any other way. But he saw it, and gave leadership to mend it, taking the pain upon himself.

I walk for campaign finance reform, which we surely need if we are to have a democracy of self-governing, free people—not the wage slaves of a corporate state. And while we fight, we must have ground to stand on, and that ground is a broad mountain called the middle class. We cannot have a democracy without it. It is that city of hard working, equal brothers and sisters that Dr. King could see on the mountaintop. Well, we have indeed come a way up toward equality, but let us not take this day as a time of self-congratulation while the whole mountain slips into the sea, leaving nothing but deep water between the very rich and the poor.

Where are our leaders and our representatives at this critical moment, when the shape of our economy and our jobs are in the balance, and when the health of our environment is in the balance, and when everything to do with fairness and equality that Dr. King and so many others lived and died for are in the balance? Where are our representatives? They are sold and gone, I fear. Sold and gone. The lobbyists in Washington spend millions per month for their attention, and you know where that leaves you and me, don't you?

What cause do you care most about? Go to Washington to press your case, I ask you: will you be talking to your representatives, and will they be listening to your arguments and making decisions based on the best interests of our country and our world? Today, they will not, and that is the tragic condition we must not allow to persist. They are all running on high-speed treadmills of fundraising that give them time to listen only to big money lobbyists, and the latitude to do only their bidding.

For a people who have given their sons and daughters to the defense of freedom, this is unfairness on a grand, new scale. We rise against it. Fairness compels us…

The Disruption Economy

Ms. Haddock at the Cumberland, Maryland, Rotary Club on January 25, 2000. The response was wildly enthusiastic.

Thank you very much. In my walk I have seen countless main streets in hundreds of towns, and it is heartbreaking to see the boarded-up windows and empty sidewalks. Other than homelessness, of course, it has been the only sad thing I have seen, not counting quite a few armadillos and foxes and other animals that did not make it across the road as they had planned. It is sad that the economic life of our towns can be listed among the road-kills.

You, however, have done so much with your beautiful downtown, and there is such a sense of vitality in Cumberland, that I can talk about the issue here without it being a criticism. It is not your problem here, except that we are all Americans and we must all care about the vitality of Main Street America, for it has historically provided the strong middle-class soil for the flourishing of our democracy.

There is an advertisement currently running on television showing a man coming to work in the morning on a New York subway and sitting down in a small cubicle and making his first telephone call of the day to a client. He is a stockbroker. The announcer says, "If your stockbroker is so smart, why does he still have to work for a living?"

Well, that may seem like a good question, but it really is not. Working for a living is a fine idea. It is perfectly fine to make a living serving the needs of others. It is perfectly fine to manage investments so that they grow carefully over the years. It is not essential that everyone buys penny stocks and becomes billionaires overnight. A stockbroker does not have to be incredibly wealthy to be incredibly worth his or her salt. That is obvious.

So, what is really behind this ad, which of course was for an Internet stock trading service, or should I say, a casino? The Internet is only the latest tool that allows big, distant companies to put middle class businesspeople and professionals entirely out of business and to deny their clients their wisdom and caution.

Here we see an attack on the very legitimacy of a stockbroker. Who is safe from such an attack? Surely not insurance agents, real estate agents, travel agents (poor dears), retail store owners, pharmacists, bookkeepers—anyone. We are all competing with automated systems and with 25-cent an hour labor on the other side of the world. Which members of our middle class can survive? And how can our democratic society survive without a strong and stable middle class? As that television ad shows, the demonization and undermining of our local professionals and our town economies is very much underway and very well financed. Besides purchasing television ads, these Internet giants are buying our elected leaders.

Now, you're starting to understand my direction. You have been wondering, "What does all this have to do with the issue she walks for, campaign finance reform?" Look no further than the pledges the presidential candidates are now making to keep the Internet free of sales taxes—a policy that will make it increasingly difficult for Main Street merchants to compete. Then look at who is funding these candidates, and you will see the names of the same billionaire companies doing business on the Internet.

The computer-based financial management program, Quicken, which controls some 85% of the market for that sort of thing, is now selling every kind of insurance on the Internet, as a part of its software. They will soon be selling home mortgages and they are already selling investment products and banking services. If you walk down Main Street in three years, will any of your neighbors be selling insurance or mortgages? Will there be any banks behind the ATM machines? Not if the mega-corporations have their way and destroy all our middle-class jobs. Disruption is not a good thing.

Maybe there is a natural evolution involved here, but it is important for you to know that the new law that enables these companies to pull the rug out from under all the state insurance and banking regulations went through Congress last year on a fast track, greased by millions of hard and soft campaign dollars. If you are in the insurance, banking or mortgage business, ask your senators and representatives how they voted on the big financial services bill last year, and you will know if they can be bought or not. You will know if they represent your interests, of if they have sold you down the river. If they say that the bill was good and necessary, tell them that they might have some credibility if they had not taken the money from the bill's lobbyists.

The biggest problem with the current campaign finance system is that we can no longer trust our elected leaders. We don't know if they are making decisions for the right reasons, or for corrupt reasons. We have our suspicions, and suspicions alone are deadly to a democracy.

In a corrupt environment where public policy is for sale through the campaign finance system, towns and small businesses and family farms, and the people themselves, cannot successfully compete for representation. If that is the case, then a coup of sorts has taken place. We continue to finance the government with our taxes, but it no longer serves our interests or answers to our concerns. This is a change of government and a treachery to those who have sacrificed their lives and limbs for our freedoms.

Those causing this change of government—senators and representatives, lobbyists, corporations and the very wealthy—are consciously and aggressively putting us out of the picture. They are conspiring daily to steal our government from us.

Don't go away from this meeting thinking that I was speaking against the Internet. I do not mean to suggest that it is a bad thing, or that the nature of commerce should not evolve. I do mean to suggest, however, that our elected leaders should be looking to our interests, not those of the highest bidders, and that is in fact what has happened; the power center of our democracy has moved from the Capitol building to the lobbyists along K Street and Pennsylvania Avenue in Washington. I am suggesting that, in this time of rapid change to our economic system, we need our representatives to carefully represent our interests.

Hanging in the balance is the nature of our town economies. What does it matter to a community to have its own businesses owned by its own townspeople or by faraway, multinational corporations?

It is, of course, the difference between a community of free men and women, and a colony—which is rapidly becoming the condition of many American communities. The first president to really see the problem of the small business and the small farm pitted against over-large corporations was that wonderful Republican, Teddy Roosevelt. He broke up the trusts while he was in power. The minute he left power, no leader took his place to defend the human scale of our communities, and to defend the health and breadth of the middle class. This battle has been untended for most of the last century. So, we have watched the decline of the family farm, the decline of family businesses, the deterioration of towns, and a growing income gap that leads rather directly to personal stress and family stress and all they bring.

It may seem that I have picked on the Internet a little bit, so let me say something to cheer up the Internet people in the room before I close. There is a dark and light side to every new thing. Yes, it will challenge us to find new ways to be free communities where people own and operate their own businesses, but it allows anyone, including the parent or elder at home and the smallest of small businesses, to provide services or products to a worldwide market. That can help he middle class, if it is nurtured in that way.

Another bright side of this new invention is its potential to provide a new medium for political campaigning: one that can potentially be free of charge to candidates, or nearly so, and a means of collecting small contributions that can overpower the billionaires.

All this can, and surely will, revolutionize politics in America. The Internet is only one case. There are many new things we can do to move into a better future, but we the people must be in the driver's seat. The interests of ordinary people must be represented, which is not our situation today. If you will go down this hill to Washington without $100,000 in your pocket and try to get your representatives to listen openly and help you on the basis of what is right, why, you are dreaming. I remember a time when you could do that without a penny in your pocket, and they were interested to listen and take action. I witnessed it many times.

Thank you very much, and I do hope you will push your representatives to support the campaign finance bills now before Congress.

Don't Give Up the Ship

> *Also, in Cumberland on January 24, 2000, after a good portion of the townspeople and their children birthday-marched with her through town, Doris delivered a speech from the back of a caboose in the town's rail station. It was her ninetieth birthday:*

Thank you all very much indeed. What a wonderful birthday this is, here in the exquisite setting of historic Cumberland, Maryland. It is such a treat to be in a place even older than myself.

President Washington, I have recently learned, was here in 1794 to review the federal troops sent here to discourage a little rebellion called the Whiskey Insurrection—a disagreement over the advisability of a tax on distilled spirits levied by the rather new federal government.

President Washington noted this in his diary: "After an early breakfast we set out for Cumberland—and about 11 O'clock arrived there... I passed along the line of the Army; & was conducted to a house, the residence of Major Lynn of the Maryland line... where I was well lodged, & civilly entertained."

Well, I know how he felt.

That residence, by the way, is just over there, across the way where we can see it, still standing, against all odds, to which I can also relate. But we see how the past is cherished and respected in Cumberland.

We must also cherish and respect the institutions that provide, after long and bloody years of defense, our freedoms as a

self-governing people. I am headed to a city where those institutions are being sold for scrap—a place far downhill from here.

But before we depart from this place, let us look around at the beauty of America. Let us look at a town where there is no other way for public servants to be except honorable. If a mayor or constable or executive of such a town as this should sell out the interests of his townspeople for the sake of a campaign contribution, a career would be over, and shame would come to a family. This is the real America. Down the hill is another America, where there is no shame, and where the buying and selling of America's interests are not called bribery, though that is what they are, and where the stealing of real power away from what we founded as a government of, by and for the people is not called a coup or a treason, though that is what it oozes toward.

So, we Americans stand here no longer concerned about the tax on our whiskey. We can bear that; we can even drink to that. But we cannot bear the greater damage that is being done to us by far more intoxicating poisons: power, money, and prestige: distractions that blind the vision and poison the souls of those within the Beltway in an epidemic of disdain for the American People—whom they take as a mere market for their political products—chiefly their darling selves.

A flood of special interest money has carried away our own representatives and our own senators, and all that is left of them—at least for those of us who do not write $100,000 checks—are the shadows of their cardboard cutouts. If you doubt it, write a letter to them and see what rubber stamp drivel you get back. For all we know, they might all have died ten years ago, and the same letters continue to be sent out.

Now, standing here on the back of this charming caboose, why would I spoil my own birthday party with a bunch of politics? Well, because I love politics, and this is my party.

I love it to death, and I shall love it to unto death. It was the dinner table meat and potatoes of my wonderful, 62-year marriage. It is what we talk about in the town halls of our communities and on Tuesdays in my reading group, which we call the Tuesday Morning Academy. It is what self-governing Americans must hold in steady fascination and endless conversation, if we are to be free.

My husband, Jim, died several years ago after a ten-year struggle. At the end, he said that he was ready to go and that he did not want any more food or water. It took him eleven days and nights more, before he was successful. My son, Jim, my grandson Raphael, sat with him at night and I held his hand during those last heartbreaking days. After ten years of caregiving, it is difficult for an old wife to adjust, especially when the mate was such a sparkler—such a person of light and life and red-blooded activism. He was fun. And how do you wake up each morning in a world where the fellow you would run to with a new thought to share is nowhere to be found and where he does not answer your call through the house?

My dear friend Elizabeth died too, shortly after Jim, and also after a long period of caregiving that did wear me out.

I am not trying to make anyone feel sorry for what happens in a long life. All things end. But I want to say something important about it, and that is why I bring it up. I stand here on the tail end of a caboose. And so it was when Jim and Elizabeth were gone. Life seemed very much over—all the picnics, all the hikes, all the frosty ski trips. I was deeply depressed, and I know that many people today are in that same place. And what I want to say to them, and for all of you to remember for that day ahead when you think you are standing at the end of your life, is, damn it, don't give up the ship.

I know I am mixing my transportation metaphors with trains and ships, but it is my 90th birthday and I have just walked 3,000 miles and I shall mix metaphors as I please.

For those of you who have lived a long life and think you are finished with it, I tell you that, if you will pray for courage and look to the needs of your community rather than yourself, a great energy and happiness will come to you. Indeed, your community needs your wisdom and your patience. Your family needs you, too, whether or not they believe it. And your country needs you.

Friends, look at this country, our genius republic—this great sailing vessel we have built so that we might find our way to the future together as free and equal citizens—as friends and partners in self-governance. Though it is centuries old, the paint still smells new some days, and the flags still snap in the wind. But what a price we have paid for it! I do not have to remind you of the rows upon rows of marble stones that mark the sacrifices our friends and our children and our forefathers and mothers have made to build this great craft and keep it safe, do I?

But now, in a time when people are so stressed in their lives and are so unaware of what it means to truly live well—to live free, to live with enough leisure and confidence to be the stewards of their own lives and communities—in this time, we strangely find ourselves having to explain why it is a bad thing if multinational corporations control our elections, and why it is a bad thing if our elected leaders no longer represent the interests of the people.

I know that some of these people just need to be awakened. We can do that. We can show them a future they will want. But there are others who know very well what has been lost in this nation over the last few decades and they have lowered their fists slowly in despair. To them, to my generation and the generations younger, I cry to you, please—don't give up the ship.

Work with us to return our self-government to the human scale. Help us defeat those Members of Congress who will not take even the first step toward reform, which everyone with a brain and a soul knows is the simple act of outlawing the huge money contributions that now flood our elections—special interest dollars with special interest obligations.

We care nothing for the taxes on whiskey, because they are nothing to us anymore. But we pay billions of dollars each year in extra taxes or inflation because tax breaks are being sold for campaign contributions—we pick up that tab.

Where do we march to make a fight of this? Not against our government, but against those inside and outside of it who have set up their cash registers in our temples of democracy. Where are they? Downhill from here in a place that smugly dismisses the rage of Americans.

Let them become suddenly uneasy. Let them notice that the birds are strangely silent and the dogs are barking. Something is brewing, and it is called an election. Thank you for helping me celebrate one of the great days of my life—I know that many of you have come a very long way. Let's adjourn now to make our plans for Washington and have some cake.

Note: The largest blizzard in 40 years rendered the road from Cumberland to Washington impossible for walking. Ms. Haddock used her cross-country skis to complete the 184 miles to Washington, using the snowy towpath of the historic C&O Canal. It would bring her all the way into Georgetown.

As Senator McConnell had said campaign reform would pass Congress when "hell freezes over," Ms. Haddock had a photo of her progress on skis sent to him with her compliments.

Entering Washington, D.C.

> On *February 29, 2000, Ms. Haddock was met by approximately 2,300 people at Arlington National Cemetery, where she began her final miles to the Capitol Building, by way of K Street— Lobbyist Row. Reformer Jim Hightower, equipped with bullhorn and high spirits, led the big crowd across town. Ms. Haddock paused at the Lincoln Memorial to give the following remarks:*

The beauty of this memorial we take from the ancient Greeks. Inside this temple of democracy, however, sits no god of Olympus, but a man of Illinois—a country lawyer with a talent for self-government, which we all must share if a government of the people and by the people and for the people is not to perish from the Earth.

We all have our own religions to guide us, but we share a common civic belief, and this is a temple of that shared belief—the belief in our ability and our responsibility to manage our own government as a great people. It is our belief in the proper human scale of things. We have sculpted Mr. Lincoln large in stone, but only so that this solitary man might not be dwarfed by the columns of our institutions, and only so that we might remind ourselves that those who would  overwhelm any of our individual voices in matters of our self-governance with their money or with the very power we have granted them, are the opponents of all good things represented in this place.

If our experiment in self-government is to survive in reality as well as in name, we must defend the position of the individual. That is what we march for today, and Mr. Lincoln's enduring optimism for his people encourages us onward. So, let us now go to our own Capitol, just up the hill from here.

On the U.S. Capitol Steps

> *Ms. Haddock's arrival remarks, delivered on the East Steps of the U.S. Capitol to the 2,300 people who walked the final miles with her; Tuesday, February 29, 2000, after welcoming remarks by many Members of Congress and reform leaders:*

Thank you. Before the days of the Civil Rights Movement, a senator might have said that the millions of oppressed people were happy in their condition. But now, after so much history, after so much painful growth, we see the insensitivity and ignorance of such a statement. How did anyone dare think that the oppressed and abused were happy in their condition?

Before the rise of the Environmental Movement, a senator might have looked upon a polluted Hudson River and said that the old river is simply paying the inevitable price for progress. But

now, after so much sickness endured, so much new understanding gained of our fragile network of life, and after so much effort by so many, we see the insensitivity and ignorance of such a statement. How did anyone dare think that our beautiful land stretches itself out for companies to ravage for their profit and our misery?

Before the Campaign Finance Reform Movement, which grows every day now with such power that it shakes the political parties to their foundations, a senator might have advised his fellow member to not worry about voting down campaign reforms, because the people don't care. That is, in fact, what Senators McConnell and Lott did say—and that is what precipitated my walk. I have come to tell them that they are wildly mistaken, and I am glad to have you along to add your voices to mine.

This morning we began our walk among the graves of Arlington so that those spirits, some of whom may be old friends, might join us today and that we might ask of them now: Did you, brave spirits, give your lives for a government where we might stand together as free and equal citizens, or did you give your lives so that laws might be sold to the highest bidder, turning this temple of our Fair Republic into a bawdy house where anything and everything is done for a price? We hear your answers in the wind.

What might we call the selling of our government from under us? What might we call a change of government—from a government of, by and for the people, to a government by and for the wealthy elite? I will not call such a change of government a treason, but those more courageous shadows standing among us, whose blood runs through our flag and our history, and whose  accomplishments are more solid beneath us than these stone steps, why they might use such a word in angry whispers that trace through the polluted corridors of this once great Capitol and slip despairingly through the files of correspondence and receipts in this city of corruption.

Senators, we speak for these spirits and for ourselves: No, you may not have our democratic republic to sell. What our family members died for, we do not forget. They died for our freedom and equality, not for a government of the rich alone.

Along my three thousand miles through the heart of America, which I made to disprove your lie, did I meet anyone who thought that their voice as an equal citizen now counts for much in the corrupt halls of Washington? No, I did not. Did I meet anyone who felt anger or pain over this? I did indeed, and I watched them shake with rage sometimes when they spoke, and I saw tears well up in their eyes.

The people I met along my way have given me messages to deliver here. The messages are many, written with old and young hands of every color, and yet the messages are the same. They are this: Shame on you Mitch McConnell and those who raise untold millions of dollars in exchange for public policy. Shame on you, Senators and Congressmen, who have turned this headquarters of a great and self-governing people into a bawdy house.

The time for this shame is ending. The American people see it and have decided against it. Our brooms are ballots, and we come a-sweeping. We will visit every state where anti-reform Senators are up for reelection and bring with us the long lists of your corruptions, and I will be with them. You will try to buy your way out if it with expensive advertisements. But we will take such spending as further proof of your corruption, for Americans pay ten dollars in extra taxes for each dollar you receive for your campaigns from special interests.

While we are here to speak frankly to our representatives, let us also speak frankly to ourselves: Along my walk I have seen an America that is losing the time and the energy for self-governance. The problems we see in Washington are problems that have been sucked into a vacuum of our own making. It is not enough for us to elect someone, give them a slim list of ideas and send them off to represent us. If we do not keep these boys and girls busy they will always get into trouble. We must energize our communities to better see our problems, better plan their happy futures, and these plans must form the basis of our instructions to our elected representatives.

This is the responsibility of every adult American, from native to newcomer, and from young worker to the long retired. If we are hypnotized by television and overwrought by life on a corporate-consumer treadmill, let us snap out of it and regain our lives as a free, calm, fearlessly outspoken people who have time for each other and our communities. Let us pass election reforms and anti-corruption measures in our towns and cities and states, winning the reform wars where they are winnable, changing the national weather on this subject until the winds blow even through these old columns.

Now, Senators, back to you. If I have offended you speaking this way on your front steps, that is quite as it should be; you have offended America and you have dishonored the best things it stands for. Take your wounded pride, get off your backs and onto your feet, and go across the street to clean your rooms. You have somewhere on your desks, under the love letters from your greedy friends and co-conspirators against representative democracy, a modest bill against soft money. Pass it. Then show that you are clever lads by devising new ways for a great people to talk to one another again without the necessity of great wealth.

If you cannot do that, then get out of the way—go home to some other corruption, less harmful to a great nation. We have millions of people more worthy of these fine offices.

So here we are, Senators, at your doorstep: We the people. How did you dare think we do not care about our country? How did you dare think that we would not come here to these steps to denounce your corruptions in the name of all who have given their lives to our country's defense and improvement? How did

you dare think we were so unpatriotic to have forgotten all those rows upon rows of graves that mark how much we, as a people, care for our freedom and our equality?

The People of our nation do care. They have told me. They laugh with disgust about you on the beaches of California. They shake their heads about you in the native village of Hashan Kehk in Arizona. In Toyah, Texas, they pray for deliverance from your corruption. In Little Rock, they understand in anger how you undermine their best dreams for our society. And in Memphis and in Louisville and in Chillocothe and Clarksburg, through Pennsylvania and Maryland and into this city today, the people see you for what you have become and they are prepared to see you another way: boarding the trains at the great train station down the street. They are ready for real leaders, unselfish and principled leaders who will prove their worth by voting for meaningful campaign finance reform this year.

The time has come, Senators, for reform or for some new Senators. Tell us which it will be, and then we will go vote.

In the name of the people who have sent me along to you, and in the name of the generations before who have sacrificed so much for the sanctity of our free institutions and who stand with us in spirit today, I make this demand.

> *Note: Nearly two years elapsed before the passage of the reform bill. During this time, Ms. Haddock covered the nation with her speeches and rallies. At critical moments she returned to the Capitol for direct action, including a four-day, 24-hour walking fast around the Capitol Building in freezing weather.*

Taxation Without Representation

Ms. Haddock's spoke to a community audience in Harrisburg, Pennsylvania on March 13, 2000—she was in town to support a reform bill in the state legislature. Though she was ready to go back to New Hampshire for a rest, she agreed to this important detour.

Friends, we taxpayers find ourselves shouldering the burdens of the nation while wealthy special interests are able to avoid paying taxes, shifting their share, plus many of the costs of their own businesses, including environmental cleanup, onto working people. This goes quite beyond taxation without representation, for the problem is not so much that our interests are being neglected, but that our interests are being squarely attacked and damaged while we subsidize our attackers. It is un-American in all its aspects.

The dark heart of this treachery is the current campaign finance system, where special interests simply buy public policies aimed against us with their campaign donations. This is not the normal condition of our political history. This is not inevitable. It is now being practiced on an open, brazen, and massive scale, and it is cancerous to the underpinnings of a fair, free, and civil society.

One way or another, of course, we publicly finance our elections. Under the present system it is a fact that, for every dollar that commercial interests invest in political campaigns, they receive in excess of ten dollars, provided by taxpayers, in the form of special tax breaks and subsidies. That clearly is a public funding system—just not a good one from the taxpayers' point of view. There is nothing to say they will not take all of our tax money someday, as they settle into their power.

If we instead will directly fund our political campaigns, on the theory that the citizens need information about the candidates, then we can save nine out of those ten tax dollars, for we will not have to provide all the tax loopholes and special benefits that commercial campaign contributors now demand from lawmakers in exchange for their donations to candidates.

It might occur to you that another approach would be to find a new class of candidates who cannot be bought. We must, however, understand that the very best of us are soon co-opted and then corrupted by the horrible expenses of political campaigning. We must stop putting good people in ethically corrosive environments until they become, like Senators Santorum and Specter—financial monsters who rail against reform and care only for the next grotesque donation of blood money to keep themselves half-alive. They do not represent their people anymore.

We have allowed this horror to happen. It is up to us, you and me—for that is what we mean by democracy—to design elective systems that will bring out the best in our people. It doesn't matter if our systems are a little expensive. There is no reason why we should pay more for our roadways and our parks than for the institutions that provide us fair representation, freedom and equality.

Those are my thoughts on public funding, which I hope, if you do not agree with, you will at least think about. Now let us briefly consider soft money donations. Friends, how would you feel if you were involved in a lawsuit and you found that the other side was making big financial contributions to the judge just before the ruling?

How would you feel if you were a baseball player in the World Series, and you found that the other team was making big financial contributions to the umpires?

How would you feel if you were a citizen in a free democracy and you found that the person elected to represent your interests was receiving huge financial contributions from people outside your district whose interests were completely opposed to yours and those of your community?

Is there a fundamental difference between these situations? I don't think there is.

And now, would it matter if the contributions to the judge were not made directly, but were instead made to the judge's family foundation and passed back to the judge?

Would it matter if the political contributions were made to the elected official's party, and then passed back to the official?

Well, in the last example, those unregulated, or soft money political contributions tend to be in very high amounts— quite beyond the reasonable limits imposed on donations made directly to candidates. Even a child can see that this back-door approach is wrong and unfair. And there is no reason, so long as the Supreme Court says that contribution limits are legal, why such deceptive practices should be allowed under the law.

That is the clear logic of it, and here are the feelings I carry to this issue in my heart. I have lived long enough to see great sacrifices made by a great many people to preserve our freedoms in a nation of equal citizens. People who try with their wealth to steal our representatives from us are attempting to steal our freedom. For this we have gone to war and have sacrificed the lives of our children. Do they think we will permit it now for some reason? We will not.

Maintaining our freedom is constant work, and it is our business here today. Some, like Senators Santorum and Specter, will stand in our way. But they stand against our history as an equal and free people, and they stand against the tide of this reform.

In this reform battle, you and I fight for the position of the individual, for ourselves, for our friends, family and neighbors, and we fight so that those who gave their lives to the defense of our equality and freedom did not do so in vain.

I support the important work you are doing here. You are patriots to the cause of the American experiment in self-government, and I urge your fellow citizens to join you.

> *Note: Associated Press story by George Strawley, 3/16/2000: DATELINE: HARRISBURG PA. Doris Haddock, a longtime activist nicknamed "Granny D" who trekked from Los Angeles to Washington to show that everyday people were interested in changing how political campaigns are funded, put in an appearance Monday on behalf of the bill. And on Tuesday, the House reversed an earlier vote and approved the bill to allow taxpayers to "check off" their approval of publicly funded campaigns for governor and lieutenant governor... Wearing a straw hat decorated with a turkey feather and a vest adorned with pro-reform buttons, the 5-foot Dublin NH woman climbed the Capitol steps with legislators and addressed television cameras inside the building. Longtime advocate Sen. Allen G. Kukovich, D-Westmoreland, said it was the most attention he has seen given to a reform-related event in years. The proposal approved Tuesday calls for a system of public financing.*

Good to be Home

At a welcome home event in Peterborough on Saturday, April 1, 2000:

Thank you. It is good to be home. My long walk took me through so many landscapes and communities that I often could not imagine that the parade of them would ever end.

America is a very large place indeed, and yet it is a small town. We are a close people—closer in temperament and bound by a deeper friendship than we give ourselves credit for. We love being Americans more than we love being of any town or city or state. We have not only our history in common, but our dreams. And our idea that we can all be free, that we can treat each other fairly with justice under the law, and that we might all find some happiness and prosperity together, while it is not unique to America, is certainly not the common condition or attitude of the world.

So, I come home full of new admiration for our American family.

I am thankful for the encouragement of my townspeople and family, who supported the idea of my walk without regard to my age and who allowed me to take my own risks. Some of you went to great trouble to come walk with me, which was such a joy.

I have not come home to die. I have come home to live robustly, pursuing my civic interests and my dream of a democratic republic where ideas, work and honorable service are the currencies of exchange, and where bribery is shamed into near extinction.

Wherever I went across America, people were so glad to meet someone who just simply cared. They were happy to meet someone who listened and who had something to say, but who was not running for something or trying to get some personal advantage from it.

If any of you would like to ever run for office, I will tell you that if you will cast self-interest into oblivion—to use a phrase from our original Iroquois Constitution—people will follow you anywhere. What they are tired of, in all departments of life, is selfishness. There is no reason why an old lady walking down the road should have been so well received, except for the fact that it had been a long time since any of these people could go meet someone who was not a callow, self-promoting, snake oil-selling political promoter. They wanted to shake my hand and wish me well, not because they thought I was something special, but because I was someone like them.

Americans are not selfish. They are kind and full of a great spirit. They want and they merit leaders who will cast self-interest into oblivion.

We Americans are idealists, but we are practical. We are not waiting for Gandhi to come walking down the path to represent us with perfect, unselfish honor. We will make the best of who we have, as we always do. We have no perfect neighbors, no perfect family members, no perfection in ourselves, and we mustn't expect it in our leaders or our candidates. Yes, we must accept the fact that they do not suffer from low self-esteem. We must take them on as a project—like a woman takes on a man with potential—and we must make something of them, especially if they will at least express their willingness to learn and to improve, and to deepen and widen their political souls.

But for now, I'm glad to be home. Thank you all.

Her additional remarks in the Dublin Town Hall, up the hill from Peterborough and walking distance from her home in the woods:

Thank you. Coming back home after my long journey fills me with thankfulness. I am thankful for the love you have extended to me during my time away. No distance, it seems, is so far that the heartstrings of home cannot find us and comfort us. Your willingness to encourage me, write me, come walk with me, and to come here today and welcome me back into the bosom of our town is an act of love that touches me deeply.

I am thankful to my family members who made my adventure possible in so many ways. I especially thank my son, Jim, who did not dismiss my idea as some further sign of my aging, and who in fact set out to make my dream a possible one.

All along, he provided, like Dorothy's ruby red shoes, my magic way home if things should have gotten too hard. But, thanks to him, they never did.

I am thankful to the memory of my husband and my friends, whose spirits and memories urged me on and who now stand among you to celebrate me home. I am thankful for so many kind Americans and visitors from other nations whom I met along the way and who sheltered and fed me and shared their lives with me. You simply cannot imagine the moral richness of this land. We are blessed in many ways, but mostly with the company of our fellow Americans.

I am thankful to our God, who let a million sleepy-eyed drivers see my small frame on the margins of dawn roads and Who sent me good weather or at least tolerable weather each day. He never sent me anything He had not prepared me for as a woman of New Hampshire—even the snow.

Yes, I am indeed thankful to New England, for it raises its children with business-like severity so we might be a little tougher and more courageous, and so we might become, after long years here, great connoisseurs of beauty in everything.

My travels for my political issue are not over, but I soak in this homecoming and I delight in this exchange of our neighborly love and friendship.

We Are Problem-Solvers

Ms. Haddock's remarks to the New Hampshire House, in their chamber, April 18, 2000:

Thank you very much. I want to honor the pragmatists in this room. It is easier to be a political idealist, and to refuse to budge because you know you are right… Idealism always sounds better than it actually works out. Pragmatism, if it is based on love and mutual respect, usually takes us to the happier place.

Just sitting there and being idealistic requires no further work. In politics, it is the best excuse for laziness and the easiest road to finding useful enemies, against which you can raise money and votes from the similarly narrow-minded.

It takes more maturity to be pragmatic. In fact, I believe the very definition of maturity is the ability to accept and even embrace a lesser evil so that life can move forward.

Now, this principle could apply to any of our most difficult political issues today, for many people are willing to let a great deal of harm go forward so that they can defend the absolute rightness of their opinions—opinions that are usually better argued in a holy place than in a public place.

But I would like to apply the principle today to the public financing of our elections.

I know it rubs many people the wrong way. But let's be practical for a moment and consider our circumstances. Yes, we all believe in free speech. As a people, it is our most cherished freedom. That does not mean that we tolerate speech that causes a crowd to panic or speech that is wrongly and purposefully damaging to a person's reputation. We have a pragmatic approach.

Public financing, some say, might damage free speech in elections. If we are pragmatic, we can prevent that from happening. We can have voluntary programs that do not compel people to participate, for example. If the program allows more candidates to participate and to get their ideas out to the public, that is a net gain for political speech and worth the work of developing a program that suits our main concerns. In the states and cities that now have public financing as an option, the number of candidates is increasing. As they will not have to be on a fundraising treadmill after they are elected, they will be freer to speak their own mind, and they will have more time so that their constituents can speak freely to them. Those are huge net gains for free speech in a democratic republic.

But some people may oppose it because public dollars are being used to support political positions they might not agree with. This is also true, of course, when a town has a speakers' stage built for the candidate forum in the park, or when a ballot is printed up, or when an incumbent is allowed to send newsletters to constituents, and on and on. Just as our streets are not built to bestow a benefit on any one person who might happen to be using them, so a system of information about candidates is there to serve the larger goal of a well-informed electorate. Surely we can be pragmatic about this. The candidate's picnic in the park, sponsored by the town, can be our mental model, though we use the more modern public address systems now provided by television, radio, newspapers and the Internet.

Now. Let's honestly look at how our fellow citizens now regard government and political leaders. To a certain extent, we always hold our government and our politicians at a disdainful distance. That may be part of our defense mechanism that allows us to maintain our personal freedom and our objectivity as voters. But if it goes too far—if too many people are up in the canyons with their ammunition and their direct satellite links to God or Rush Limbaugh, then we risk losing those freedoms by backing away too completely from the fact that we are supposed to be a self-governing people who are, ourselves, the American government. Some pragmatic space in the middle is necessary. **How do we make more of our people feel connected to the processes of self-government?** Can public funding of elections be a tool for that necessary task? Well, the pragmatist inside you is saying, "possibly so," and that it the right answer.

The day may come again when ordinary people can afford to advertise their campaigns without spending a fortune, and the day may come when broadcasters and newspapers do a better job of telling us all about the people running for office. In the meantime, we pragmatists are confronted by the fact that it is too  expensive for most people to proceed upward as our community leaders. They must sell their souls or spend their children's inheritances, and neither is right. If we want freethinking and accessible public servants, we know that we must take all this money out of the way. It stands between us and our representation.

I congratulate you on your practical approach. More and more states and cities are solving this problem by creating public financing systems that address most people's concerns.

As New Hampshire people, we have a tradition of free speech in our town halls and in these rooms. Let us be among those states that look to the future with pragmatism and with a love for the very idea of political speech unfettered by financial strings. Thank you very much.

Her remarks inside the Capitol Rotunda

Friends, the First Amendment to the Constitution says that Congress shall make no law abridging the freedom of speech, or of the press, or the right of the people peaceably to assemble and to petition the Government for a redress of grievances.

We are peaceably assembled here, in this our hall, to freely speak, to petition our Government. Our grievance is that we no longer have proper representation. Our elected leaders are consumed by the need to raise election funds from special interests, and they no longer are able to represent the needs of the people or of our ravaged Earth.

We must declare our independence from the corrupting bonds of big money in our election campaigns by reforming our campaign finance system. We must alter our government. As a people, we know how to declare our independence and authorize alterations of our government. Here is how we did so in Congress, July 4, 1776:

"We hold these truths to be self-evident, that all men are created equal, that they are endowed by their Creator with certain unalienable Rights, that among these are Life, Liberty and the pursuit of Happiness. —That to secure these rights, Governments are instituted among Men, deriving their just powers from the consent of the governed..."

While she was reading from the Declaration of Independence, Ms. Haddock was arrested and manacled by Capitol Police. Tourists, who had been applauding, seemed shocked. She was taken to jail with 29 supporters.

Her later court pleading:

Your Honor, the old woman who stands before you was arrested for reading the Declaration of Independence in America's Capitol Building. I did not raise my voice to do so and I blocked no hall.

The First Amendment to the Constitution, Your Honor, says that Congress shall make no law abridging the freedom of speech, or of the press; or the right of the people peaceably to assemble, and to petition the Government for a redress of grievances, so I cannot imagine what legitimate law I could have broken. We peaceably assembled there, Your Honor, careful to not offend the rights of any other citizen nor interrupt the peaceful enjoyment of their day. The people we met were supportive of what we were saying, and I think they—especially the children— were shocked that we would be arrested for such a thoroughly wholesome American activity as respectfully voicing our opinion in our own hall. Any American standing there would have been shocked. For we were a most peaceable assembly, until Trent Lott's and Mitch McConnell's police came in with their bullhorns and their shackles to arrest us. One of us, who is here today, was injured and required a number of stitches to his head after he fell and could not break his own fall. He was detained for over four hours without medical care. I am glad we were only reading from the Declaration of Independence—I shudder to think what might have happened had we read from the Bill of Rights.

I was reading from the Declaration of Independence to make the point that we must declare our independence from the corrupting bonds of big money in our election campaigns. And so I was reading these very words when my hands were pulled behind me and bound: "We hold these truths to be self-evident, that all men are created equal, that they are endowed by their Creator with certain unalienable Rights, that among these are Life, Liberty and the pursuit of Happiness. —That to secure these rights, Governments are instituted among Men, deriving their just powers from the consent of the governed, —That whenever any form of Government becomes destructive of these ends, it is the Right of the People to alter or to abolish it."

Your Honor, we would never seek to abolish our dear United States. But alter it? Yes. It is our constant intention that it should be a government of, by and for the people, not the special interests, so that people may use this government in service to each other's needs and to protect the condition of our Earth.

Your Honor, it is now your turn to be a part of this arrest.

If your concern is that we might have interfered with the visitor's right to a meaningful tour of their Capitol, I tell you that we helped them have a more meaningful one. If your concern is that we might have been blocking the halls of our government, let me assure you that we stood to one side of the Rotunda where we would not be in anyone's way. But I inform you that the halls are indeed blocked over there.

They are blocked by the shameless sale of public policy to campaign contributors, which bars the doors and the halls to the people's legitimate needs and the flow of proper representation. We Americans must put an end to it in any peaceful way that we can. Yes, we can speak when we vote, and we do. But we must also give our best effort to encourage the repair of a very broken system. We must do both.

And the courts and prosecutors in government have a role, too. If Attorney General Reno would properly enforce the federal bribery statute, we would see lobbyists and elected officials dragged from the Capitol Building and the White House, their wrists tied, not ours. I would be home in New Hampshire, happily applauding the television news as my government cleaned its own house.

In my 90 years, this is the first time I have been arrested. I risk my good name—for I do indeed care what my neighbors think about me. But, Your Honor, some of us do not have much power, except to put our bodies in the way of an injustice—to picket, to walk, or to just stand in the way. It will not change the world overnight, but it is all we can do.

So, I am here today while others block the halls with their corruption. Twenty-five million dollars are changing hands this very evening at a fundraiser down the street. It is the corrupt sale of public policy, and everyone knows it. I would refer those officials and those lobbyists, Your Honor, to Mr. Bob Dylan's advice when he wrote: "Come senators, congressmen, please heed the call. Don't stand in the doorway, don't block up the hall."

Your Honor, the song was a few years early, but the time has now come for change. The times are changing because they must. And they will sweep away the old politician—the self-serving, the self-absorbed, the corrupt. The time of that leader is rapidly fading. We have come through a brief time when we have allowed ourselves to be entertained by corrupt and hapless leaders because they offer so little else, and because, as citizens, we have been priced out of participation and can only try to get some enjoyment out of their follies. But the Earth itself can no longer afford them. We owe this change to our children and our grandchildren and our great grandchildren. We need have no fear that a self-governing people can creatively and effectively address their needs as a nation and a world if the corrupt and greedy are out of their way, and ethical leadership is given the helm.

Your Honor, to the business at hand: the old woman who stands before you was arrested for reading the Declaration of Independence in America's Capitol Building. I did not raise my voice to do so and I blocked no hall. But if it is a crime to read the Declaration of Independence in our great hall, then I am guilty.

Judge Hamilton's sentencing remarks:

"As you know, the strength of our great country lies in its Constitution and her laws and in her courts. But more fundamentally, the strength of our great country lies in the resolve of her citizens to stand up for what is right when the masses are silent. And, unfortunately, sometimes it becomes the lot of the few, sometimes like yourselves, to stand up for what's right when the masses are silent, because not always does the law move so fast and so judiciously as to always be right. But given the resolve of the citizens of this great country, in time, however, slowly, the law will catch up eventually. So, it becomes my lot to apply the law as it is at this time—perhaps not as it should be, but as it is. With every confidence that, to the extent that it is lacking in righteousness, it will reach that point eventually given the resolve of her citizens to make it right." (He sentenced them to a few dollars and time already served—the better part of one day in jail—and released them. He asked to meet with them in his chambers. He shook Jim's hand and gave Ms. Haddock a hug.)

> *Note: an email: "I have just read this account. I am a French citizen, but I was moved. It feels like a Capra movie. That is the America that the world wants to love, the America we French went bankrupt helping win the War of Independence. Years ago, when I was serving my 12-month tour as a conscript in the French army, I was posted in a mid-18th Century building that once housed the Ministry of the Navy. It is on Rue de l'Independance Americaine - American Independence Street - right across the street from the great Palace of Versailles. History has its addresses, and sooner or later they will whisper in your ear. God bless Doris Haddock and the true ideals of America. – Philippe Dambournet*

The Seven-Layer Cake

Ms. Haddock delivered variations on this speech at a number of schools in New England. This version was delivered at Franklin Pierce in the spring of 2000.

Thank you. I am honored to talk to you all today. I know you have worked hard to get to this moment, and I admire you for that. Life is so much more complex and fast moving than when I went to school, and things were already hard enough then. I would like to try to give you something of value in my brief remarks today—some piece of useful knowledge that perhaps you weren't taught in school or at home, and something easier to hear from someone who has lived a long time.

It is the simple fact that the world as it was back when I was your age is still with us, and you live in that world, too. And the world of several hundred years ago is also still with us, as is the world of the misty, prehistoric past. We live in a many-layered world, and we are many-layered people. Each era of our history makes a contribution to the way we live our lives, and each era imposes expectations upon us, to this day. Unless we understand that fact, we will have a hard time navigating through the conflicting rules and expectations of life. Think of life as a seven-layer cake and you will do all right.

As an example, I have often overheard young men arguing about how difficult women are to deal with. Are men supposed to open a door for a woman or not, pick up a check at a restaurant or not? Aren't they supposed to now treat a woman as a total equal? They are confused because they don't understand that a person is not one thing. A person is many layered. There is certainly a very old layer where women are princesses and men are princes, and that layer needs to be acknowledged sometimes when the moment is right, and a carriage door needs opening. That layer is still with us and it glows under the moon. There is also of course a modern workplace layer, where men and women are colleagues or employees and where they treat each other in a businesslike way, without reference to gender, and where it is a great sin to open a door for someone instead of an opportunity.

And there is, of course, an ancient, biological layer that compels a man to seek a mate and compels a woman to find the resources for a safe and respectable home. This is just one layer, but it must be acknowledged and given its due. And because it is one of the oldest layers, it is the first one you come across as you approach maturity. Though you may not believe me, there is more to life than that layer.

There are also layers, of course, from our own childhood, still intact, still demanding comfort and security and the freedom to creatively explore.

So, you must look at a person and see all of this, if you are to see truly—which is to say, wisely.

When we make snap judgments about people based on some single quality, we dehumanize them, and that is a moral crime, indeed. I know you have probably had the experience of being in the same activity with someone and getting to know them, even though you never might have talked to that person on your own. But you became good friends or at least you came to respect each other. That happened because you got down a few layers with that person.

Most people are worth knowing, if you will take time to understand them. Unfamiliarity with other people, ignorance of other people, is what makes war possible and violence possible, and it drives all the social divisions in a school or in a town or a nation or a world. When you understand people well enough, you can't help but love them, even if you hate them, too. If you think those are incompatible emotions, I remind you to think about your relationship with almost any close family member.

Understanding people is loving them. Hatred is what we feel when we do not understand.

Are there some people so over the top with their evil deeds that they do not qualify for this sweeping statement of mine? Some people may take more understanding than we are capable of summoning. We must accept our own limitations.

One of the most difficult and important tasks we have as humans is to regularly, and sometimes without cause, forgive each other and move ahead with our lives together. If one layer of someone's personality flares up and causes us harm, we must try to put it in perspective among all the other layers of that life.

A long marriage requires the willingness to do that, time and again. No relationship can long survive on the basis of what happens in just one or just a few of those layers. Understanding and forgiveness require a view of the whole person.

That whole view can also help us to forgive ourselves. It is a great act of maturity, I think, to not condemn yourself or define yourself by what goes on within just one of these different layers, some of which are intensely biological or set down in cement in early youth. Sometimes we are given to suddenly see with great clarity an amoral and reptilian side of our own motivations, but it is wrong to think we have suddenly discovered our true self. That one layer is no more important than the layers of loving kindness, so long as the negative layer is not given free rein.

Emotional maturity is the ability to stay balanced, not letting any one layer dominate our lives. I do not mean that we should fiercely suppress the darker layers, for to do so causes us to transfer our fear and loathing onto other people. But we must give every layer an opportunity to go for its walk at a time when it will do least harm. And our more positive layers we must of course encourage and put in the company of like souls, for the most important thing we can do for ourselves is to surround ourselves with people we respect for the best reasons—we simply cannot help but become like the people around us.

After acknowledging and coming to understand the layers of life, a gentleman may finally come to know when to open the door for a lady and when to share a check. A woman may come to know that a fellow is more than the polygamous forest creature he sometimes seems—he is also the artist and the prince, the poet and the friend. It is not easy, of course, to negotiate through all the layers lain down through the eons of evolution and the rise of civilization, but if life were easy it would be a bore. Life is that seven-layer cake, and so are our hearts.

The icing on top is not youth or victory or wealth, but a measure of enlightenment and love that comes as we live with our eyes and minds and hearts wide open.

I wish you a happy life. I hope you have a high opinion of yourself, that you understand that you are worth the trouble you have invested in yourself so far, and that you are worth a continuing investment in a future that begins always at this moment.

If you feel alone in the world, or at work, or at school, or at home, here is something you can do: approach someone you thought to be unapproachable and ask them how they are doing today. See what happens. Our alienation, which is the greatest danger to us all, is not so hard to overcome with a little honest curiosity about the situation and the feelings of the person just over there.

I hope you will look to the people around you—in your family and your community, and your nation and the world—with an open heart and an active curiosity, so that you may not condemn but, instead, better understand and befriend them, and so that your friendships may mature into love. Thank you.

In the studio of
Democracy Now!
In New York City

The Bribery Coast

In the company of politicians, musicians and reformers, Ms. Haddock' spoke on the West Steps of the U.S. Capitol on September 19th, 2000. Following her remarks, she marched with Georgetown students from the Capitol to the Justice Department, where she pasted a copy of the existing federal bribery statute on its front door. Her remarks on the West Steps:

Thank you very much. Do you think there are enough of us here, that if we all wished the same wish, it might come true? Well, let us try. Let's imagine that we could pass a law that could work some magic. It would get big money out of the way of our democracy.

The law would read as follows:

"Whoever directly or indirectly, corruptly gives, offers or promises anything of value to any public official with intent to influence any official act; or, being a public official, directly or indirectly, corruptly demands, seeks, receives, accepts, or agrees to receive or accept anything of value personally or for any other person or entity, in return for being influenced in the performance of any official act, shall be fined under this title or not more than three times the monetary equivalent of the thing of value, whichever is greater, or imprisoned for not more than fifteen years, or both, and may be disqualified from holding any office of honor, trust, or profit under the United States." Unquote.

Now, how hard must we wish to make that law the law of this land? Humor me, please, and close your eyes tightly and click your heels together three times. One, two, three.

You have done it. The law I read to you, condensed somewhat, is indeed the law of the land. It is United States Code, Title 18, Chapter 11, Section 201: Bribery of public officials.

18. 11. 201! Under the crystal-clear provisions of this law, most of the people who make laws in these buildings should be in jail. Under the unambiguous provisions of this law, political parties that extract protection money from industries are in violation of federal bribery law, and they require prosecution.

I ask our Attorney General to investigate the sale of public policy by the elected leaders of our nation, to investigate the purchase of public policy by the great lobbying operations that have set upon our temple of self-governance like great vampire bats.

18, 11, 201! The law is there to be enforced, and the evidence drips from every window of K Street, flows down every hallway of Congress, rises waist-deep in the fundraising ballrooms of every luxury hotel in this city, washes in waves from the Bribery Coast that K Street has become.

How many good men and women have died for our freedoms as a self-governing people? Go across the cold river to Arlington and see! The spirits of the dead, and the hearts of the living are filled with sorrow for what now happens in this, our own Capitol, home of our democracy.

Title 18, Chapter 11, Section 201! That must be our demand at the door of Justice!

Corporate Leadership

At the suggestion of Bill Moyers, Business for Social Responsibility invited Ms. Haddock to speak to their 800 members in New York City, November 8, 2000. It was not strange for her to be in their company; she had been New Hampshire's highest-paid woman executive in her time.

Thank you very much. I am delighted to be in the presence of so many people who care deeply about the serious issues of our day and who are striving to make important changes. I believe the brightest business leaders—those capable of planning three or four chess moves ahead—are reformers by necessity, for there can be no sustainable commerce without a sustainable Earth, and there can be no free enterprise and no enjoyment of the fruits of enterprise without sustainable democracies to guarantee those freedoms.

I set out on my walk across the United States at a time when the leaders in Congress were saying that no one cared much about campaign finance reform. I wanted to demonstrate that I indeed cared, and I hoped to meet others along the way who also cared or who might become interested. That was indeed what I found.

Not very many people understood the term "campaign finance reform," but nearly all of the thousands of people I met felt and still feel that they no longer have senators and congressmen who represent their interests.

They believe that wealthy special interests have taken away their opportunity for a representative democracy. And many, many people got teary-eyed or they cried outright about it. They sent me on my way with a prayer for success for all of us, and many of them—over 2,000 of them—came to join me for the last mile in Washington, D.C. That was a joyful day, but despair, sadness and anger were the typical emotions I encountered along my way.

On that last day of my walk, we started from the graves of Arlington—rows upon rows of white stones that mark the sacrifices that have been made for the idea of freedom and self-governance. I felt those honorable spirits walking with us to the Capitol to demand an end to the political bribery that now dominates Washington. The present bribery nicely calls itself campaign finance—much as prostitutes might wish to be called personal companions—but it is what it is.

We gave witness against it on the Capitol steps and later from the very Capitol Rotunda, where some of us were arrested and jailed for peaceably assembling and petitioning our government for the redress of our grievance. I had very good company in jail, by the way, including young people from some very notable families, as Mr. Moyers may be aware.

My long walk was a 14-month, 3,200-mile opportunity to think about what cures might apply to this corruption. Time and again, people agreed that the full public financing of our campaigns is the only real way to ensure that ideas and character will count again in our politics. I was surprised to hear this opinion voiced from progressive California to conservative Texas, Arkansas and West Virginia. People are so truly sick of the present system of special-interest-dominated politics that they are ready for that change.

I was surprised to learn about the public financing of campaigns during my walk. I was not informed about it when I began. People along the way convinced me that there is no other chance for real reform.

Four states have already embraced public financing of campaigns. A candidate for the Arizona legislature, for example, needs to find 200 people living in his or her district who will contribute no more or less than $5 each. All further campaign funds are provided by the state clean elections fund. No special interests need apply. It worked beautifully in the election cycle that concluded yesterday.

In Arizona and in Maine, Massachusetts and Vermont, the citizen listening to a candidate at a neighborhood forum can now, for the price of $5, be the one and only fat cat in the system. That is a breath of fresh air for democracy, isn't it? It is a victory for the human scale.

I am certain that public financing will also come to our federal elections. We have it in a modified way now for our presidential elections, but the presidential candidates who take the federal funds are not restricted from raising and spending other funds, which is a problem.

What else will drive the success of this reform? Well, the continuing damage to the weather system, to the healthy diversity of nature, and to the healthy diversity of local economies, I believe, will create a rising demand for effective leadership and proper representation without interference from selfish interests unconcerned for the future.

I know you are here because you are reformers. I am sure it gives your efforts some urgency when you hear that the polar ice cap is a third thinner than it was in 1980, and that animals are dying off at a rate that qualifies our age as the planet's sixth major extinction. I am sure that you must be ready—if you have not already done so—to add your own voice to those demanding serious action on these fronts. I doubt that you would waste your time on window-dressing issues while these fundamental issues of global consequence are filling the streets and the jails with young and old protesters around the world. We do not want to repair our representative democracies for the fun of it; we see urgent issues that are not otherwise being addressed properly.

A young carpenter from Chicago, Nick Palumbo, who helped me across a good many states in my recent walk across the U.S., and who more recently helped me across Missouri in my walk there for Missouri reform that concluded last week, was one of the many young people who peaceably protested in Philadelphia during the Republican convention. He cares deeply about non-violence and went all the way to India to study its principles from the followers of Mr. Gandhi. He was nevertheless jailed in Philadelphia for no good reason and held for ten days under purposefully brutal conditions. If you want to know why many Nader voters would not compromise to support Mr. Gore, it is because an entire generation is becoming radicalized against corporate-dominated politics, and it is just beginning. It grows with every change of weather, and it grows as every big-box discount store destroys another Main Street of family businesses—and I walked through hundreds of such ruined communities. It is the human scale resisting the scale of the monstrous, and history has shown that human scale always wins in the end…

There has been a power race between business and

government, and neither side can afford to unilaterally disarm. So, you may feel the need to own a few dozen senators, because the government can make or break your business.

But the game has gone on now to a point where half the people don't vote and the other half aren't too happy either, because they don't think it's a democracy so much as it is a rigged game of special interests. That is what sends people to the streets instead of the ballot boxes. How do you step back from this brink without putting your company at risk?

You do it with courage. If you need a role model, Arnold Hiatt ought to do fine for you. He was the second largest individual political donor in the 1996 election. But he saw that, long term, political giving is a losing game.

Let me quote him exactly; Mr. Hiatt said:

"Breaking the link between candidates and big donors would inevitably contribute to a more equitable, and efficient, allocation of our country's ample resources. Wasteful subsidies that serve narrow economic interests rather than the national interest—like the $500 million a year subsidy that goes to the sugar lobby, or the tax break for ethanol producers that has cost taxpayers more than $7 billion since 1979—would wither away. Instead, government would probably find the money to subsidize, for example, every child in need with high-quality day care: many studies have shown that every $1 spent in quality day care saves $7 in later remedial costs."

He continues: "Such changes in our spending priorities would help create a healthier and more productive work force, and a better climate for business in general. I've seen this occur with individual companies and I'm convinced it can occur on a wider scale. This is not only a moral imperative—it is good business sense. The well-being of a company cannot be separated from the well-being of society." Unquote Mr. Hiatt.

I agree with every word he said. Further, the less involved corporations become in government, the easier it will be to reduce the size and cost of unnecessary government.

Now, in the shorter term, if you are concerned that your withdrawal from political participation will allow other business interests to take your place, let me remind you that you can head them off by supporting the full public funding of elections.

Now, I'll bet you thought you had outlived or divorced all

the old women who would dare nag at you like this. But I love free enterprise at the community scale and all that it brings to a free world. We all, whether we are major stockholders or customers in line, have an interest in a healthy system of commerce. We have that in common.

Further, you and I share a deep feeling for all those who have given their lives to defend our freedoms and our government of, by and for the people. We know these brave souls—many of whom we knew and loved—did not die so that special interests might steal away our representative democracy. Part of you cares more about that than your business profits, and I tell you that you must listen always to that valiant voice within yourself.

When you are my age, it is the only voice still worth listening to.

Thank you for the privilege of meeting you and speaking with you, and good luck in your meetings here today.

Freedom from Anger

> *Ms. Haddock's remarks to a massive gathering in Washington's Dupont Circle, Saturday, January 20, 2001—the morning of George W. Bush's first inauguration.*

Thank you. There are many angry people in America these days, and there are many things for them to be angry about. Anger is the normal and healthy reaction to unfairness, criminality and injustice.

But, as I am young enough to yet see with my own heart, let me tell you that there are sufficient injustices in the world to keep us angry all the time, unless we give ourselves some freedom from anger, and it is only with that freedom that we can truly improve the world.

As I am old enough to have seen and felt a third of our nation's history, let me tell you that there has always been a sufficient supply of raw deals to keep us toasty warm with rage, if we are only capable of rage instead of action.

So, if you find yourself one day in charge of a company or a community or a kingdom, and you discover that you now have enemies who would try to bring you down, here is your best strategy: keep them angry about little issues so that their energies will be spent before they get to the big issues that could truly threaten you.

You can lead a revolution from anger, but you cannot lead or govern a democracy from anger. You will fail miserably and create great harm.

Anger is not the engine of our democracy. Our imperfect Union, our ever-wobbling Republic, beset as it is by occasions of demagoguery, corruption, assassination, poor judgment and faulty elections, moves generally forward toward greater human kindness, greater fairness, greater equality—all riding on the shoulders of brotherly love.

Our nation moves upward despite all its errors and deficiencies, because it is a society founded upon an inspiring common dream that has proved durable. The dream has moved us forward. Indeed, America is a fairer, more just place than it was 91 years ago, when I was born.

What is the real issue today? It is the fight to hold to that dream of representative democracy, for how can we serve each other's needs and preserve our very Earth if we are not at the reins of our own democracy? There's the issue, friends: not the theft of an election by one Supreme Court justice, but the larger theft underway of democracy itself through the financial corruption of political campaigns…

Let us fight to win, but with only as much anger as we need to sharpen our resolve.

We shall do it for all who have given themselves to the betterment and the defense of our great idea: a government of people, for people. We shall do it for our children and grandchildren and great grandchildren, who need for us to be brave and take action at this critical moment.

You know from your own experience that, once you step onto the street to oppose a great injustice, a joy comes over you because you are representing your deepest values. That joy is at odds with your anger. So, let the joy win the battle; joy is more powerful than anger in changing things.

And change things we must, so that our great Capitol building might be filled with the warm light that ever streams from the hearts of our people. Thank you.

This, My Government

On March 19, 2001, a year after her arrival speech on the U.S. Capitol steps, Ms. Haddock returned to Washington to picket the Capitol Building as the Senate began debate on the McCain-Feingold bill. She decided more drastic action was in order, and so planned a 24-hour walking vigil around the Capitol Building for as many days and nights as the debate might continue through the following week. The weather was not cooperating; freezing rain in the 20s was predicted for the coming days, and she was asked by those traveling with her to cancel the walking fast, especially as her emphysema had been giving her coughing fits, and pneumonia was a clear risk. "Well, I'll certainly need a good Mackintosh," she replied, and took a cab to an army-navy surplus store, where she bargained for a heavy one. She then sent this message to her supporters:

Friends: Mr. McConnell and some other senators are of the opinion that Americans do not care about campaign finance reform. It is true that many people are unfamiliar with that term. They are quite familiar, however, with the fact that their government has been sold out from under them by wealthy special interests. If they seem uninterested in the selling-out of the very democracy their friends and family have died to defend, it may only be because they despair of a solution, given our present Congress.

I do not despair. I think these men and women who serve in our Senate are capable of doing the right thing—of lowering the boom on soft money and holding the line on hard money. We know that many of them care. We have seen them working hard on this matter these past days.

If the senators need some encouragement—if they need to know that Americans indeed care—then let the few of us who can afford the time to be here do more to show we care. Let us walk continuously around our Capitol, day and night, while the Senate struggles to free our democracy from the corrupting clutches of big money. While they are doing their best, we will be doing our best with this walking vigil.

Those at home, I hope, will call their senators again and demand the passage of McCain-Feingold in a way that will outlaw soft money—huge contributions given by corporations to parties, who then pass it to candidates—and preserve the existing $1,000 limit on hard money contributions—the money given directly by individuals to candidates. Yours, Doris

> On March 24, 2001, the Saturday before the planned Monday action, she met with a group of 25 college students who came to Washington to lobby for campaign finance reform as a strategy for protecting the environment. Here are her remarks to them, delivered on the West Steps of the Capitol. Her speech draws upon an earlier speech given in Little Rock during her long walk. After the meeting the students joined her in picketing the Capitol Building.

Members of the press and many elected leaders say that the people do not care about campaign finance reform. Mitch McConnell says most people care more about static cling.

Part of my mission in walking across the country was to see if this is true, and if it indeed was, to talk to people to help them to understand the seriousness of our situation as a people.

What I found was that very few people knew what I was talking about when I used the term "campaign finance reform," but nearly everyone agreed that they no longer have representatives in government, and that their representatives have been bought away from them by big-money interests. So, they do care a great deal about campaign finance reform—often they care to the extent that their eyes fill with tears; but they did not have a name for this abandonment they feel so deeply.

Now, good political reform work requires that we look deeply into our reform issue and see how it connects to basic cultural values.

For example, if you have a great-uncle who was killed in the Second World War, or an uncle who was killed in Vietnam, you might wonder if their spirits are angry when they see the country they fought for moving from a democracy of the people, to an oligarchy where the interests of only the elite are served. Of course, they did not die to protect the interests of the super-wealthy and the corporations, while school children go unfed and innocent people rot in corporate jails.

So, as I walked, I connected campaign finance reform to the memory of these people. I think I first did it in the little desert town of Salome, Arizona. I recited the war poem, *In Flanders Field*.

Now, what we are talking about is the element of sacrifice. You rarely can have successful reform politics without an element of sacrifice. Here I was in Salome, talking about the sacrifice of others. But, about eighty miles earlier in my trek, as I finished walking the Mojave Desert and arrived in the river town of Parker, Arizona, the mayor (Sandy Pierce), took me all over town talking about the sacrifice I had just made, and that made people interested in my cause.

In the same way, it was hard for me to get signatures on my petition at the very beginning of my walk as I stood on a sidewalk near the ocean in Santa Monica, until a kind woman joined me and told passers-by about the sacrifice I was about to make. That made them care enough to stop and sign.

Gandhi and King taught us, of course, that we must take the pain of social change upon ourselves, if we are to change society. If we inflict it instead upon other people, we have not changed the world for the better, and we shall only generate short-term and very unpredictable changes. It was King's nonviolent work that gave us the voting rights bill and other civil rights bills, for example. All the riots and other violence gave us short-term programs that did more harm than good in the final analysis.

So, our own willingness to demonstrate the importance of the issue, by inconveniencing ourselves in a dignified way that our fellow citizens can relate to, is our most powerful tool for change.

Sometimes you have to be willing to get arrested, but there is no percentage to be gained by harming anyone or anything, as that goes beyond what the people can accept and see themselves doing. The whole point of reform politics is to attract, not repel, the supportive thinking of the people.

The teaching of nonviolent political action is a five-fold technique that we must always remember. It must be remembered wherever people gather with the intention of improving their community or their world. Here are the five steps:

Number One: Determine the truth of a situation before taking a strong position. If it is an injustice, can it be clearly documented? Bring in the experts if you can. Be sure what you are advocating is actually and demonstrably the truth.

Number Two: Communicate your findings, your position and your request for change in a respectful and achievable way to the people who have the direct power to correct the situation. Don't ask someone for something they don't have the power to give. Don't shout on the sidewalks if you have not yet communicated respectfully with the parties in authority and have respectfully waited for a reply.

Number Three: If the response does not come, or is insufficient, bring public attention to the issue. Work openly so the thinking process of the entire community can be engaged. Gandhi and King were accused of staging events for the media. Of course they did. Social change is a public process, and it does not happen for the good when it happens in the dark. Engage the

community openly so that they can be a part of the debate and the decision. Openness works easiest in a democracy, but it also works in authoritarian regimes, so long as there is visibility between the action and the public. Few governments, no matter how authoritarian, are immune from public sentiment.

Number Four: If those in authority will not correct a very serious situation that must be resolved, despite an open airing of the issue, then the advocates must be willing to make sacrifices to demonstrate the seriousness of the matter. When King marched forward toward baton-swinging policemen in Selma, he showed that the issue was important. When Gandhi led marches and gave speeches that he knew would lead to his imprisonment that day, and when his followers stood in long lines to be clubbed by security forces standing in the way of their rightful path, the world stopped its daily routine to inquire: what injustice motivates the self-sacrifices of these people? What, in fairness, should be done? And here is the difficult key to success: It is in the endless willingness of the advocates to make a continuing sacrifice that guarantees their victory. No injustice is powerful enough, or has enough supporters, to stand against the flow of such generosity.

"You have been the veterans of creative suffering," Dr. King told his followers in his "I Have a Dream" speech. Well, creative suffering is something we all have the power to do. It happens to be the most powerful force for change in the world. It is always in our pocket, ready for the call of our conscience.

There is a fifth step, made necessary by the fact that the non-violence technique, when properly practiced against moveable opponents, always wins. The fifth step, as developed by Mr. Gandhi and as practiced by Dr. King, is to be gracious in victory—to remember that your enemy is your brother, and that you should therefore settle the dispute kindly, accepting some compromises and granting as much face-saving courtesy as possible to the other side. You will meet again, after all, and why not as friends? Gandhi said on many occasions that we have to love and respect our adversaries because they are our brothers and sisters and also that they are parts of ourselves and of our God. He meant it.

Here is a passage from his autobiography:

"Man and his deed are two distinct things. It is quite proper to resist and attack a system, but to resist and attack its author is tantamount to resisting and attacking oneself. For we are all tarred with the same brush, and are children of one and the same Creator, and as such the divine powers within us are infinite. To slight a single human being is to slight those divine powers, and thus to harm not only that being but with him the whole world."

Dr. King believed much the same, and you can hear it clearly in the "I Have a Dream" speech, where he calls us together as "all of God's children."

These are the five steps that gave India its freedom and which gave America its second revolution of independence at a moment when it could have devolved into a full race war. The moment King left this world, the violence that could have been ours all along showed itself in Watts and Detroit and a hundred other cities and towns. There is no courage in a thrown bottle of gasoline. Courage is what we saw in the buses arriving at Little

Rock's Central High School and in the Selma march, not the riots of so many cities. Good changes, like the voting rights act and the opening of universities and public facilities, came from King's work. Poor changes, temporary changes, came from the anger of riots.

Love works. Love wins. Love endures. It is our religion, and it must also be our politics.

In my walk across the country, I speak against the idea that those individuals and those corporations with the greatest wealth should be able to buy our elections and our candidates and our representatives, diverting their attention from the needs of the people, and preventing honest candidates from winning.

That we have a problem, that money has become more important than ideas in our political debate, is a proven fact. That this huge, national influence-peddling scheme results in a mass diversion of the public wealth from where it is needed to where privileged people would have it for their own use is no longer a debatable point. When I walk with this message, I have the advantage of speaking the simple truth, proven by every major research institution, on both the right and left of political life, who have taken the time to investigate the issue.

We have asked those in power to remedy the situation, and for a long time they refused. We sacrificed. We gave ourselves up for arrest. We—thousands of us—kept the pressure on, thought it cost us time and energy and our meager incomes to do so.

And this coming week we shall see something for it. It will not be much. We will get rid of soft money. We will take that hill, thought we will pay a high price for it, as I am sure they will try to raise hard money limits in the process. We will do what we can to limit that damage. Thank you. If you will lend me a sign, I will join your picket of this gorgeous building of ours.

As the McCain-Feingold Bill debate began inside the Senate on Monday, she launched her action with a small speech to a gathering of Members of Congress and her supporters at the Senate "swamp:"

Thank you, friends. The fact that the American government is my government is a joy to my heart, even if it does not always feel like my government. When it is, it is a part of me and I am a part of it. I help direct its actions according to my civic values, through the work of my representatives in its powerful councils. In this way, through them, I can better fulfill my responsibility to do good for my countrymen and for others around the world. If I cannot fulfill these responsibilities, a soul sickness comes over me and over the land itself.

There is a high price paid in America and around the world when Americans, whose values are profoundly fair and generous, are not in control of their own government and when they do not believe they are indeed a self-governing people.

Some of you have never known the feeling that it is your government. Some, by income or race, have been denied that feeling through all their generations. But I have been lucky—privileged is of course the better word—to often feel it was my government.

And so, some may think I do not see the same world as do they.

They may say, "Doris, did you not see how the credit card industry bought a bill last week?"

I saw that. All America saw that.

Or, "Doris, did you not see how manufacturers stopped the worker safety bill, or how the coal lobby has undermined our nation's ability to stop the destruction of the Earth's climate?"

Yes, I see that. I agree with you—the challenge is great. Indeed, there may have been uglier Congresses in our history, or less competent, but there have never been more fundamentally corrupt Congresses than these in our time. Certainly, democracy had a better chance of survival in the darkest days of the two world wars than it does today, at the hands of the campaign corruption from within.

But I am not worried: I know we shall overcome this time of destruction.

It is a bit early to celebrate. I do hope that, at the end of this present battle for reform, we can say the day is ours. But we are small and the forces against us are strong and unprincipled in battle. Before this week is out, they may take our best garden tools for reform and twist them into blades to dig corruption even deeper. They may make a nice plum pudding of the McCain-Feingold bill. In any case, it will be something to watch.

They will cry into their million-dollar campaign troughs over the idea that any real reform might tilt the playing field unfairly, though it doesn't matter how the field it tilted if no team is playing for the people. The playing field is tilted up beyond the moon now, and it matters very little to ordinary Americans whether it is tilted in favor of the credit card party or the coal party, as neither is playing for us.

But I am not discouraged. We the people can afford any losses and yet always overcome. We are the millions. Ours are those who have happily died to defend this country and its idea of a government of its people. We the people are generous in our sacrifice for democracy, and no one is rich enough or cruel enough to stand forever in the way of our sacrifices and our aspirations for our country and our world.

It will be written in history that America came into a dark time when its leaders became corrupt—so dishonest they could not admit it even to themselves.

And history shall further record that a dedicated band of people sacrificed the best years of their lives to set their people free from the bondage of corruption. Let history say they did so, or that they died trying.

I know these heroes by name and many of them stand around me now, and I know that the spirits of those who sacrificed everything for democracy walk behind us—bandaged, on crutches, but each wearing a determined smile because they understand that we are not interested in forgetting their sacrifices for self-government. They walk with fife and drum, reminding us that heaven may be our work tomorrow, but America is our work today. And as long as any one of us is left standing to claim these columns, to claim this, my government, then we are not defeated.

Thank you and join me now—those of you who can and are dressed for this weather—as I begin my walk and vigil.

As she walked around outside of the Capitol Building in the hard weather, Matt Keller, John Anthony, Dennis Burke, Claudia Malloy, Nick Palumbo and others worked the halls of the Senate, urging Senators to meet with Ms. Haddock, "so we can get her out of the cold." In this way, she met with half the Senate, usually asking nicely for their vote but sometimes offering to walk across a senator's state to oppose them if they voted against the bill. At least one vote changed on the spot, and others changed due to the pressure of phone calls from Ms. Haddock's now-thousands of followers—she had also been on national television, urging viewers of NBC's Today show and ABC's Good Morning America to call their senators. The 24-hour fasting walk continued for four days. She stopped only for brief respites in a brownstone behind the Supreme Court, home of Bill Moyer's son, John. She would consume only vitamin water suggested to her by Dick Gregory, a veteran of many political fasts. In that way—Gandhi's way of self-sacrifice—she helped get the bill passed by the Senate.

She had sent formal invitations to tea "under the trees" to each senator by hand, providing her volunteers a way to approach the Senate offices.

She was called by Senator McCain to stop walking and be in the gallery when the final vote was taken. It still had to go to the House, but it had now passed the Senate—over McConnell's energetic efforts to defeat it.

Witness report by Ben G. Price, national organizing director for the Community Environmental Legal Defense Fund, writing in the Alliance for Democracy newsletter (used by permission):

> Senator Arlen Specter is Cordially Invited to Tea with Mrs. Doris Haddock Under the Trees in the Lawn between the Senate and the Supreme Court at any time or hour from Tomorrow Morning, Wednesday, March 1, 2000 at 11:00 a.m. onward for several days or until everyone has an opportunity to take a stand for or against campaign finance reform.

"It was a blustery, rainy gray day in Washington, D.C. We were joining Doris Haddock, better known as "Granny D," as she continued her 24-hour walking vigil around the Senate.

"While the hundred senators debated the McCain-Feingold bill that would ban "soft money," Granny D walked around the Capitol grounds to emphasize her outrage over the selling of democracy by its supposed representatives. She had walked 3,200 miles to demonstrate her commitment to reform; now she was circling the Capitol, day and night. When I caught up with her she was out there in a cold rain, her signature straw hat with its feather on her head, planning to continue her walk until the Senate voted for reform.

"Lou and Patricia Hammann, of the Alliance for Democracy, were with her when we arrived. Patricia, concerned about Doris's health, asked her to consider ending her vigil.

"" When I started this, I knew it might do me in," Doris said. This was the day—Thursday—that the opposition would have its last chance in the Senate to kill McCain-Feingold outright. Senators Bill Frist (R-Tenn.) and John B. Breaux (D-La.) had proposed an amendment to invalidate the whole bill if any section, phrase, or word of it was found unconstitutional.

"By invitation, Granny D took a break and entered the Senate gallery to witness the proceedings. We joined her, gaining *entry to the mezzanine just as Senators McCain, McConnell, and a few others were making the final arguments. Then the roll was called. Lou and I tried to keep track of the votes as they dribbled in. As we watched the senators appear and disappear from the cloakroom, the tally trickled in, running two to one for the deadly amendment.*

"Across the gallery from us sat Granny D. After all the miles, all the footsteps, all the aching joints, there down below her, in the theater of the Senate, these men and women would decide whether she had walked in vain.

"At last, the decision was in: 57 senators voted to kill Frist-Breaux and 43 senators voted in favor. Mitch McConnell took the floor, obviously shaken. He saw the adoption of McCain-Feingold as the demise of political parties, since they could no longer command the huge slush funds called "soft money." Passing the bill, he said with his usual arrogance, was "a stunningly stupid thing to do." If the bill finally passed, there would be a court fight at once, "and I will be the plaintiff," he told the emptying chamber.

"Even if McCain-Feingold is passed by the House and signed into law, it will be an imperfect bill. It does not guarantee the primacy of citizens as sovereign in the electoral process. It

simply eliminates the grossest forms of obvious impropriety in the funding of election campaigns. But for the first time since 1974, something had happened."

Doris Haddock was 90. She still had three great political adventures ahead: winning in the U.S. House, a brilliant voter registration campaign and an improbably delightful run for the U.S. Senate.

The Monster at the Door

Ms. Haddock's remarks in Florida, June 16, 2001, to a voter rights meeting of young activists in Tallahassee:

Thank you. Born in 1910, I lived through 90 years of the previous century: two world wars and uncounted smaller conflicts, massacres, tortures and atrocities. Over one hundred million people died in those years due to the abuses of power that arose because governments had become disconnected from the basic human values of their people.

Our imaginations are not dark enough or twisted enough to fully comprehend the mass horrors that have been perpetrated upon the people of the world—men, women and little children; if we knew it all and remembered it all we could not draw another happy breath.

In America we are more blessed. We have come to expect that our neighbors will not be rounded up en masse and shot. We have come to expect that we will not ourselves be dragged out of bed and sent away to death—though these things do happen here, especially to our immigrant neighbors. While we may distrust an election or a party, we have—most of us—not lost faith in the good intentions of our democracy, writ large. It is balanced between left and right, and between politician and bureaucrat, and we mostly manage.

We look around the world. We understand that it is the absolute power of institutions out of balance that allows atrocities, because force is the opposite of sensitivity and accommodation. Force is a monster, a man-eating, woman-eating, child-eating beast that we keep in check but never really kill. In America, our dear Constitution is the amulet we wear to preserve ourselves from its teeth.

Our Constitution gives us our democratic republic, which has as its intention the fragmentation of power, keeping the exercise of force as close as possible to the human scale, and letting its power accumulate only where absolutely necessary for the common good of the people. The parchment document of the Constitution is not enough—we also require supportive institutions and customs; we need these five things:

1. We need fair and accurate voting systems that we can trust beyond a shadow of doubt;

2. We need worthy candidates who represent our interests and values and who are free from compromising financial or other obligations;

3. We need a free press that takes as a sacred trust its duty to inform the citizenry on the great and small issues of the day;

4. We need to be an unhurried society, with each of us given the time and resources to be active citizens, not hamsters on corporate treadmills;

5. We must be an educated people, forever students of the vital issues before us and of the history, art and literature that shapes our human sensibilities and our civic and cultural values. We require all that if we are to be a wisely self-governing people. Our schools must produce citizens. Our immigrant arrivals must be made into informed citizens.

In many of these five areas we are now in trouble. The stakes are very high, for the monster of force is never far from the door. It comes in quickly. If I told you that an unrepentant U.S. Navy seriously roughed up a Member of Congress because he was peacefully protesting, or that a building full of people who were making political puppets were summarily arrested and taken away, or that people walking calmly down the street near a political convention were arrested and brutalized for two weeks, what country would you think you were in? If I told you that I was arrested for calmly reciting the Bill of Rights in the U.S. Capitol building, and that I cried when the police tried to pull from my finger a wedding ring that had not been removed in sixty years, where would you think you were? All these things—and many more—have happened under the American flag within the last twelve months.

If I told you that a man would be in the White House who lost the popular vote, what country would you think you had landed in?

It happens quickly and moves swiftly. It is nothing for the forces of raw power to discredit the proper law enforcement agencies and set up new ones run by political cronies, with prisons and police of their own to suppress and arrest those who dare investigate or protest. It is nothing for raw power to thumb its nose at the interests of world peace or the Earth's environment for the sake of power and plunder. It can happen quickly. It can happen in America. We must have our eyes open for it and our voices ready!

Those who speak out first—the leakers, whistleblowers, activists, patriots—will be vilified, jailed, or worse. Stick up for them. Oppose the autocrat at every turn. You will be among a new generation of American patriots putting yourselves at risk to preserve our dream of individual and civic freedom. Nothing is more important than this work, as the history of the previous century shows us—clearly written as it is in the blood of one hundred million people.

To those who died for democracy we owe a sacred trust. For those who died for lack of democracy we owe our efforts to make a world worthy of their memory. **Democracy is worth a great deal of trouble and all our human strength.** Thank you.

Old Elijah's Tree

Ms. Haddock's June 24, 2001 remarks at Dublin Community Church, where she was asked to deliver the sermon—her first, not counting her speech in Little Rock's First Baptist Church; the Bible verse of the day was 1 Kings 19:

Good morning. Much is expected of us. We have not been sent into this theater of the soul to watch passively. We are not the audience but the players in this drama, writing our parts as we go, so that we might learn something—both as individual souls, and together as the fragile web of consciousness that sparkles over God's creation. It is all evolving, we hope, toward some unity with the Divine.

This life is not a test or a drill or an accidental light opera: Much is expected of us. Some days it is quite too much, indeed. Some days, everything we love is suddenly gone, or has turned against us. We look at our life and our meager accomplishments and we sense that the game is lost; the play has run; we have no more to give; we have no interest in fighting on.

So it was, so many centuries ago, when Elijah sat down to die under a desert broom tree. His own fear had chased him into the wilderness. He had fought hard and well against the enemies of the Lord, but the altars of his beliefs lay in ruins and he was the lone prophet facing heartbreaking work ahead. He had fought so long and given so much strength to his calling that there seemed nothing left inside him. When Jezebel threatened his life, he broke and ran.

And any young person who has tried to do well in school or on the field, and any parent who has tried to be saint and provider to a family, knows Elijah well, as do I. We have often sat down with old Elijah under that desert tree, just wishing it were over.

As Elijah slumbers under the tree, the Lord sends an angel

twice to nourish him with bread and water and encouragement. "Get up and eat, for the journey is too much for you," said the angel. The Lord did not send solutions to Elijah's problems—only enough sustenance so that the show might go on. For much was expected of Elijah, as much is expected of each of us.

Deep in a cave, which is where we indeed go when we have had enough, Elijah listened to the voice inside him that he knew to be the voice of the Divine. He prepared himself for the approach of the Divine itself. The wind blew until the mountain nearly fell in around him—the rocks crashing into bits. Then the earth rumbled, and a great earthquake rolled Elijah in his cave. But he did not feel the presence of the Divine in those signs, just as we do not feel much but fear and horror as our world crumbles around us now.

But then Elijah felt the presence of God in a gentle whisper. God asks him what he is doing there. God certainly knows the answer, but Elijah needs to remind himself who he is

and what his work is. And so, God makes him say it aloud. "I have been very zealous for the Lord God Almighty. The Israelites have rejected Your covenant, broken down Your altars, and put Your prophets to death with the sword. I am the only one left, and now they are trying to kill me too." Ah, Elijah thereby remembers: "That's who I am. That is what I am about. I can do this, even if it kills me to do it."

You may have said aloud in the privacy of that little cave called your car: "I am a parent of two teenagers. They both hate me, and they do the opposite of whatever I say, and I am terribly worried for their safety and their futures. I must express love instead of anger, yet I am screaming inside and incredibly lonely in this work. I am exhausted." Well, yes, Elijah, life is tough all over. It is supposed to be, or we shouldn't learn a thing and our souls might not grow an inch deeper or wider, as they must.

Much indeed is expected of us. But we shall always be given enough bread and water and encouragement to struggle through, if we will but rest under the Lord's tree. And a whisper may come to us; to remind us who we are and what work we have come here to do.

It is no secret among my friends in this church that, when my husband, Jim, and then my good friend, Elizabeth, died, I was quite depressed. God did not forget about me. He kept my son Jim and my daughter-in-law Libby at my side to give me encouragement and sustenance.

And there was a whisper in my ear—you may have heard me tell the story: Jim was driving me down to visit my sister in Florida. Along the road, as we sped by, was an old traveling man out in the middle of nowhere, just standing there. Soon, he was far behind us.

"Well, Doris," he nevertheless whispered, "what are you doing here?"

"Well, Sir, I have become an old woman. My husband and my dear friend are dead, but my son and daughter are alive. I used to travel with my husband as we journeyed far to help where we thought we could be useful. We drove to Alaska to stop atomic testing, you know." The old man knew.

And in saying it all, I remembered who I am, and I saw that there was still a great deal of work for me to do. And why should I care if it kills me, if doing it is my business on this Earth?

And so, the questions and queasiness that I had been struggling with, looking for a way to express my concern for our democracy—so polluted as it is by big, special interest money—came suddenly into focus. I stepped out of the cave of my depression and began to plan my work—my job.

I decided to go on the road to talk to people about our democracy, and what we might do to help it survive. Every door opened to me. My every thirst was quenched, every hunger satisfied. Whenever I needed a special kind of person for the work at hand, they appeared as if by magic. When it rained too hard, there was some earthly angel with a great, plastic tarp to walk with me. When the snow was too deep for walking, a beautiful ski path, nearly 200 miles long, presented itself. You must never doubt that you will be given what you need for this show to go on, once you accept the idea of who you are and what you must do.

Much is expected of us, but everything needed is given us, if we but have faith in the divine importance of our lives.

We have hard work to do in this life, and it can get very discouraging. It is hard work, loving each other, helping and forgiving each other, protecting the people and the ideas we care about, preserving nature, helping the millions of people who need our help, taking care of our own needs. It is hard work. Let us meet from time to time under Elijah's old tree and rest our bones. God will give us what we need to carry on.

The Road to Freedom

Ms. Haddock speaking on Boston Common on Saturday, September 29, 2001, at a reform rally and march for clean elections.

Thank you. Freedom is what we walk for today: the freedom to elect candidates who will represent us in the halls of our government, not represent the wealthy special interests whose puppet strings bind and twist our government and our society. We want representatives who don't have to spend all night raising money and all day paying favors. We want people who will listen to us, who will represent us and our needs, our values, and our future.

I know that the Clean Elections Law has been under fire in Massachusetts by politicians who would rather fund their campaigns with the same old special interest bribery. But the times have changed, and they had better listen very carefully to what I am about to say.

Much of the money that is given to parties by corporations, and then filtered down to the campaigns of politicians, is given by organizations that are increasingly owned by people around the world. It is their asset to give, most certainly, but it is global money, not American money. We can no longer have corporate money in our elections unless we will accept the idea that people from Asia, the Mideast, Europe, China and elsewhere are influencing our elections with their money. No, let us keep our elections for ourselves, and tell those anti-reform politicians to get with the program—the Clean Elections program, funding it fully with Massachusetts money and nothing else.

More important than the source of the money is the effect of the money. It buys our representatives away from us at a time when we need them very dearly.

For, what happens when we lose control of our own government? What horrors rain down upon us when our government does not represent our values, but instead those of greedy interests who do not vote here and therefore should not influence elections here?

We walk today for our freedom. But we walk, too, for the peace and justice that comes when our government is in the hands of the people—we the people. **The road of equality and justice is the road to freedom and peace.** Thank you.

Photo: Richard Avedon. Copyright: Avedon Foundation & New York Magazine

Fight Like Hell

Ms. Haddock spoke to the Arizona reform community on July 29, 2002. Her remarks:

Thank you. I am glad to be among my Arizona friends again. The last time I was here, I walked here. Many of you walked with me and helped me. I have come back to thank you. Some of you were also with me when I arrived in Washington, D.C. We are all a part of the effort to get corporate money out of American politics.

Arizona is a reform state. It didn't just start with your Clean Elections victory, by the way, or your open meeting laws or your lobbyist gift ban or your campaign finance laws that limit maximum donations and require full disclosure, or with your groundbreaking anti-gerrymandering Citizens Redistricting initiative. No, you have been a reform state from day one of your statehood. You were denied that statehood for several years because you were born in the era of the great Progressive Movement, and your proposed state constitution gave the people the power to legislate by initiative, referendum and recall. That seemed pretty dangerous to President Taft and others. They turned you down.

But Teddy Roosevelt came out to Arizona to dedicate the dam that you named for him. You got that dam, by the way, because he got most of his Rough Riders for the Cuban War from Arizona and New Mexico, and so, when he was president, he made sure that Arizona got the first big reclamation dam in the new federal water program.

So, while he was here to dedicate the dam, he told you to drop the populist stuff from your constitution, get admitted to statehood, then put them all back in, and that it would not be unmanly to do so in that fashion, as it was just politics. And, bless you, that's just what you did. And you have, ever since, been a laboratory turning out good reforms and bad governors.

The Progressive Movement, by the way—in case you haven't noticed—is back. I am glad to have lived to see two of them.

At the turn of the 20th Century, it was the abusive practices of banks and railroads and other corporations that swept reform across America. Farmers and small businesspeople didn't do that for any other reason except that their livelihoods were fully at stake.

What happened as a result of that uprising, in a nutshell,

was that the powers of government were expanded to keep the powers of the corporation in check—to keep corporations from overwhelming our human values and our ability to provide good lives for our families as free people.

What has happened in the last few years, in another nutshell, is that the government's ability to prevent corporate giantism and its abuse has been undermined and nearly emasculated for the benefit of the corporations who underwrite the political careers of their puppets in Congress, in the White House—Democrat and Republican White Houses—and in the state houses.

The crisis this time around is more dangerous, for not just our ability to prosper is at stake, but also our ability—and nature's ability—to survive at all.

Alaska's glaciers are melting. Seas are rising. Droughts and their fires sweep across our purple mountains and our fruited plains. Any mountain with coal under it is being sheared off and dumped in the next valley. More explosives are used against our mountains every day than we used in all of our recent wars—and why? So, we can burn more coal in an already carbon-saturated environment. No respected scientist any longer doubts that we are destroying the planet rapidly. We have an obligation to our children. We will have to stand in front of our Maker—will we not? —and explain how we properly cared for the great gift of life we were given—the birds and fishes and flowers of this Eden.

Even in this solar state, where is your solar energy? Your utilities are now opening another giant coalmine, this one across the line in New Mexico. What kind of madness is that? Isn't it enough that you are destroying the lives of Hopis and Navajos up on Black Mesa—destroying their land and draining their water—so that you can hear your pools and cool your doghouses?

This kind of cultural and environmental injustice and madness follows naturally from the presumption of corporate leaders—they are as shortsighted as they are greedy, and yes, I'm talking to the presidents of Salt River Project and Arizona Public Service—Tucson Electric is perhaps trying harder.

Let's pick on APS. They should be ashamed of themselves. They generate one megawatt of solar energy. That is it, of their 8,000-megawatt total. And they ballyhoo in environmental fairs and their green-this and green-that programs how valiantly they are trying. But in their annual reports they say how wonderful it is that demand is growing and that they are burning coal for nearly half their demand.

Perhaps we need to revisit the idea that utilities should

ever be for-profit corporations. Maybe they are killing us. SRP isn't better and is leading the way in coal mining. Do they get away with this because there is no political leadership, here or in Washington? Where, indeed, are the leaders?

If we had any, we would expect that they might come to us and say, "Well now, we must all conserve these resources. We must stop burning coal, which is the largest contributor to greenhouse warming, and we must move rapidly to solar and wind and other sustainable energies. We must make better cars and design cities that people can move around in without trashing the planet." These leaders of ours would tell us that our children's lives are in the balance and that we must all pull together with sacrifice and creativity, and they would remind us that there are more new jobs in a green economy than in a dying carbon one.

How can it be that this has not happened?

There is only one possible explanation: that there are people so greedy and so assured that their vast wealth will always find them a safe and comfortable place on a dying planet that they think they need not worry about the costs of their rampages, and that these people have, through distortions of our political process and real thuggery, taken over the top positions where they can use every crisis as a new opportunity to further their position and advance their power over us—stealing our freedom, stealing our common wealth, misrepresenting our values around the world and bringing us accelerating harm and misery.

Is there another explanation?

Where are the leaders who will move us toward a healthy, sustainable future?

Who will defend the health and extent of our middle class—which is the necessary foundation of our democracy? Where are the leaders who will say, "Dear People, our democracy rests on the solid ground of a strong middle class, and so we must find ways to eliminate the financial exploitation of our families— we must help them to rise, not cause them to fall."

Surely the leaders who represent our values and our interests would say this and would care about this. They would point to the big-box retail stores that destroy all the family businesses throughout a region, turning its people into greeters, and they would tell us, "The money you save at these stores is destroying your lives. Don't be bribed into destroying your towns and your fast-receding middle class."

Is there an explanation for why our leaders are not telling us this truth?

Who can lead us to a time and place where we have

power over our own lives, the resources and time to care for our friends and family, and the leisure to live proper lives under God's sun and moon?

Well, I know you are fighting these fights. But they can wear you down, as they never seem to stop coming. I want you to understand that the American Dream is not a leaky old boat that always needs fixing. It is not an old house that always needs repair. No, this high-reaching society of ours is not in trouble from its own age or infirmity. It is in trouble because it is under attack. The holes are not from age but from flaming ordnance. We are engaged in a cultural war, and we had better wise up to it and get rid of the leaders who are very clearly not on the people's side.

The corporations that have declared war on us give no quarter. They will shut down the factories we need without blinking. They will refuse us the medical care we need without

blinking. They will burn coal when the sun is all around us. They will push for growth when they should be pushing conservation. They will finance the careers of politicians who will make nice speeches to us but will participate in our destruction without blinking.

Dear friends, we have our families to save. We have our planet to save. We have our water and our air and all the creatures of nature—including ourselves and our friends—to protect. What a great and glorious fight we are in! But let us believe we are in it. We did not declare this war against corporations and their wealthy elite, but they have declared it against us. Let us go for victory. Let us limit the size of these beasts, limit their political participation and limit their ability to ruin our family business and our needed jobs. They act like dictators, not only to their own employees, but to all of us. They are a hazard to us, and they must change or go.

Can we survive without the little darlings? Yes, with some

inconveniences, of course. Can we survive if we let them continue on as they are? Clearly not. What do you do with a villain who trashes your world, threatens the peace and happiness of your town and family, and sends your children off to its selfish wars? You put its picture up in the post office among other villains. You go after it until this public enemy is caged and the world is at peace with leaders and institutions that represent the people's highest values and aspirations.

I suspect you will have to talk each other into running for office before you will have such leaders. So, do it. And work for your friends who are indeed running for office. Some of them are in this room, and this is your opportunity to do something that matters. Say you will help.

And keep Arizona's assembly line of reform ideas moving. Get going on instant runoff voting or proportional representation. Those reformers are here with a booth today. Go say hello. Go learn about what that reform can mean to you and your children in Arizona.

I know it's hard sometimes. Americans are tired, overworked, underpaid and sometimes we are filled with despair over the condition of our government and the institutions of American business. Can we save our American Dream and the free democracy that powers it? Sometimes we doubt that we have the energy to do it. We doubt that our efforts will make a difference. We are like the nearly unconscious man in a house full of gas fumes. He knows he must crawl out to survive, but he is tired and tempted to just close his eyes. But we cannot do that.

Too many wonderful people have given their lives for this democracy, this garden planet, this dream entrusted to us today. We have to find the time. We have to find the energy. We have to find the optimism to get up, stand up, and defend our Bill of Rights and the rest of our Constitution and our planet.

Be bold about it. Fight like hell for your values and our common dream of brotherhood and sisterhood on our garden Earth. Thank you.

Be Open to Your Own Genius

On September 5, 2002, Ms. Haddock spoke to the incoming freshmen at Franklin Pierce College (now University), New Hampshire:

Thank You. I know you all are grateful to be on campus and finally, safely away from all your grandparents and aunts and uncles who have been asking you what you will major in, what career you have chosen, and where you plan to retire and be buried. Older people are stuck in a view of the world that is quite rigid. You go to school—according to this view—learn a trade or profession, get married, get a house, raise kids to take your place, have a well-attended funeral, and then do your part to increase New England's insufficient topsoil. The great New England schools like Franklin Pierce are so reliably longstanding that they create a mirage of constancy, when in fact the world is changing rapidly, and the world of your parents and your aunts and uncles is being swept away.

For you, college will be a lifelong affair. You cannot learn enough here in four years to get you through your entire life. Your life will be about constant learning and growing through a number of related or unrelated careers, and that is a dramatic improvement in the condition of human beings—if life is about maximizing our potential, which indeed it is.

You will have a number of personal relationships in your life. I am glad to have had one marriage to one husband, but your life may well be quite different. While I recommend loyalty, I know the statistics.

The bright side of this difficult emotional terrain is that you will have the opportunity to experience enriching pain and you will have the advantage of essentially living several lives, to my one.

Of all the shifting sand your tent will be pitched upon, perhaps the condition of the Earth's ecosystem and its democracies will present the greatest challenge. If the great present division persists between the world's poor and rich, I assure you that you will live in a violent world.

If the great exploitation of the Earth's resources persists at the expense of sustainability, you will experience the flooding of Venice and other great seacoast cities and treasured beaches, and you will curse the generation before you that let it happen without trying harder to end the corruption and the selfish misuse of resources. But you will learn to adapt and fight for the planet's survival. Your career and your life will be about this struggle.

Yours may be the most privileged generation to ever live on Earth. I don't mean that you have soft advantages, but that you find yourself in a time when your individual contribution will have a heroic importance to the world. This may sound overblown. It may make no sense to you for an old woman to stand here and tell you that you, personally, are the hero or heroine whose actions will decide things for a troubled world. But I think that may indeed be the case. Our lives are more beautifully linked than you can imagine, and the genius of one life—and yours is a genius life—can affect all the others in unimaginable ways.

You must become the hero of your own life in any case, and that is enough for your happiness, regardless of any extension into the world.

Finding your genius is sometimes a hard trick. Sometimes it is easily spotted, embraced and nurtured. But some of you will  not find it until you are old and gray. Some of you will never find it, though it was always there for you to find, I assure you. Sometimes we see it and do not want to find it quite where it pops up. "Well, yes, I happen to be very good at that, but, Dear Lord, I don't want to be that for life."

Indeed, you may turn away from your own genius many times before it comes knocking with a baseball bat on some dark night of the soul.

Be open to your own genius. Try everything fearlessly. See what gives you energy instead of taking your energy away.

Discover the things that keep you joyfully up until 6 a.m. Sex, of course, doesn't count, because we are all geniuses at thinking about that. It's a given.

If you can't get excited about anything in the way of a first career, don't despair. Keep exploring. You are on a Grail quest, and your quest will be rewarded if you keep combing through life, looking for the thing that sparkles for you. It is there, believe me. It is your soul. It is your life's work.

Finding your soul is the great project. But it is not the only happiness to be enjoyed in your life—especially in these glory days of your youth. Take time each day to look at the beautiful lives around you. Look with love at these lives and be a force for good in them. We all need each other very much. There is no better way to find your own heart than to look with kindness to the needs of others. We cannot find ourselves except through friendship and love and serious respect for the lives around us.

So, the big question is, "what are we to do with our lives?" And the answer is this: we are to look at this life with eyes of love and find for our hands those things that bring us the most joy and curious interest. That is a simple prescription for a happy life and a happy college career. Thank you.

How the Takeover Artists Took Over

Ms. Haddock speaking before Citizens for Participation in Political Action, Boston, September 27, 2002:

Thank you. I want to begin by congratulating you for all the work you have done over the years. I know peace and justice work is often frustrating. Through the vision of your values, you see ahead to a world of cooperation and peace—a world of justice and sustainable economies and meaningful democracies. You wonder why others cannot or will not see these things or reach out for them, and why they in fact oppose the obvious good—why they take the part of the oppressors or the blinkered warhorses.

I would like us to take a few moments to consider why this work is so hard, and what we might do to move toward our common dreams more rapidly and with greater joy.

Some of you may be old enough to remember the Reagan Administration. Mr. Reagan and those around him believed in a very new kind of American hero. This new hero was a business hero—not the fellow who built up a family furniture store on Main Street and supported the Little League and the Scouts; this new hero was not the woman who worked late hours to create a successful travel agency, nor was this new business hero anything like any of the hard-working Americans who built-up our middle class, advanced our standard of living and gave us the resources and leisure for the proper civic life of a democracy with its leagues and Rotaries and Lions and Elks and VFWs and party conventions and all that glory.

No, the Reagan business hero was the corporate takeover artist.

Any regulations that might get in the way of these ruthless new capitalists were removed so that reptiles of uncommon greed and brutality might rule the Earth, which they now nearly do.

What soon happened was that all publicly traded corporations of medium or larger size had to look over their shoulders. How did a corporation protect itself in this environment from a hostile takeover? It had to close down any factories that were not earning obscene profits. Never mind that a factory had served a town well for a century, or that it provided a healthy and regular profit for its stockholders. If it seemed to be underperforming by the new hyper-greed standards, or if it could be closed in favor of opening a foreign plant that provided an even slightly higher rate of return, then, in this new atmosphere, the company was considered derelict in its duty to its stockholders if it did not ruthlessly act.

Perfectly good and profitable factories were closed. Benefits to employees everywhere were eviscerated, and staffs were downsized, outsourced, computerized, downsized again, outsourced again to temp agencies that paid no health care or retirement, and on and on until America became a very different place. The gap between rich and poor is now wider than at any time in our history. It began with the corporate raiders and takeover artists celebrated and enabled by the Reagan Administration and the Republicans.

Ours is still a wealthy nation for many people, but poverty is on the rise, and those with jobs find themselves so overworked trying to make ends meet that there is little time for family or for the joy of living. Indeed, there is very little joy left in American work life. Workers are not loyal to their companies, because companies treat them like expendable slave oarsmen, with no dignity or assurance that hard work will result in advancement or security. We are living in the harsh world invented by a handful of corporate raiders whose values were completely foreign to the fairness and moderation that had so long served as the proper foundation of American success and the American dream of plenty for all. They were not a new kind of person, for there have always been among us a few dark hearts of uncommon greed. What was new was the political permission they received for their rape and rampage, which continues.

And so, a new world devolved as if from a virus. The new business hero, a Horatio Alger on crack, did very well. The new model CEO derived from that moment—the ruthless mercenary who would come in to reorganize a company and render it takeover-proof by rendering it inhumane, or who would ruthlessly save it from massive debts created by a takeover. This executive was worth millions per year, we were told. In this way, a Darwinian system of corporate survival assured that the most carnivorous, rather than the most responsible, would rise to lead our most powerful commercial organizations. It became expected that, since the taken-over, debt-loaded companies needed warrior CEOs worth their weight in gold, then all CEOs should be paid to this new standard. This would require cutting wages and benefits and job security to all others below the CEOs, but so be it. Even public universities and professional ball teams would need these salaries, as they were the new standard.

As these mostly men—raiders and CEOs—moved to secure their wealthy status, they started buying up our politicians of both major parties. They joined the wealthy who had destroyed America's small businesses with their big-box stores, the Internet, and other machines of monopoly.

They together came to control Congress and the White House and state houses.

To survive and move up in these organizations, one must be like the boss. In Fox News, even reporters in local regions are told how to slant each story hard to the right, to satisfy the reptilian big bosses. There is very little remaining pretense of journalism within that organization. And many people stuck in those jobs, who got into journalism with the idea of doing legitimate journalism, are sick to their stomachs every working day. They would leave except that journalism jobs are shrinking;

so, they live in hope of better owners.

In this way, the right-wing leanings of a few people have distorted entire industries, including television news and radio networks. Political leaders are quickly infected in this trickle down reptilism—trickling down from the people who write the checks for political campaigns and who control enough of the political news to get them reelected.

It all trickles down further, to the weaker minds listening to talk radio and to those silly enough to spend time watching Fox News—listeners and viewers who buy the lies, who are simply suckered into forking over their own political best interests to the billionaire con artists who attempt to pick their pockets at the same moment they are pointing out others who, they say, are the real trouble makers.

Some percent of our people are susceptible to this kind of con, and they then give us problems by standing against any reasonable reforms. They have been spiritually twisted by the cheap poison of a hundred Rush Limbaughs into the angry, unthinking robots of the superrich.

On my long walk across America, a man driving a garbage truck told me that the biggest problem facing America today was the inheritance tax. I didn't have to ask him if he had a radio in his truck.

I remind you of all of this because it is important to know that the reason our reforms are difficult is not because Americans are split into two camps, conservative and liberal. It is not like that at all. There are lots of conservatives and liberals in America, but we are not the two sides of the divide. True conservatives in our country don't have many political leaders to look to with respect right now. Barry Goldwater may not be our favorite politician to remember, but even he believed that the government had no business in our bedrooms. He believed that a woman and her doctor didn't need the government's help in deciding her important issues. He would have laughed and become angry at Ashcroft's attacks on the Bill of Rights and his citizen-against-citizen snitching system. Goldwater believed that the only issue of importance regarding gays in the military was whether or not they could shoot straight, and he said so.

What we are seeing now from the far right is not conservatism at all; it is fascism: the imposition of a national and worldwide authoritarianism to enforce a narrow world view that enriches and empowers the few at the expense of the many, and that gives no respect or honor to other cultures, other ways of living, or other opinions. To call that conservatism is a crime against the memory of America's true conservatives, who might think that government ought to be less involved in life than we old liberals would concur with, but who nevertheless stood for certain values that today's right-wing leaders undermine at every opportunity.

If we Americans are split into two meaningful camps, it is not liberal versus conservative, but rather politically awake versus the angry hypnotized—hypnotized by television and other mass media, whose overpaid Svengalis dangle the swinging medallions of packaged candidates and oft-told lies.

It is done to prolong the open season on us all, as the billionaire takeover artists and their complicit minions bag their catch for the day. And in their bags are our freedoms, our leisure, our health care futures, our old age security, our family time, our village life, our family-owned businesses on Main Street, the middle class itself, our position of honor and peaceful leadership in the world, and the livability of the world itself. It will likely get much worse before we rise to make it better.

When we understand what we are up against, and where the meaningful dividing lines truly run, then our lives as reformers can be easier, because we shall know how to proceed.

And here is how it is best done:

Pull any contractor out of his white pickup truck, turn down the talk radio blaring from it, and ask him, "government good, or government bad?"

His glazed eyes will widen. "Government bad!" he will say. Ok, good; you found one to play with. Now ask him what the town might do to make it safer for kids to get to and from school, and around town when they're not in school, without getting killed by traffic or getting in trouble. He will have a million ideas. Good ideas. He has no clue that he is being government—if government is what happens when we get together to solve our common problems and to make life better for our communities.

You have broken his trance with the elixir of participation in decision-making. As evidence of this, we see progressive ballot propositions passing in presumably unprogressive states. Why? Because people are problem-solvers at heart.

Government agencies, of course, have often been the communitarian's worst enemies. Anything that smacks of bureaucratic rudeness or pushiness or counterproductive stubbornness does nothing but damage the idea that government is we the people, where we act together to solve our problems as fellow citizens. That corrosion of government really needs to be brushed out wherever it shows its pinched, gray face. Would it be possible for Progressives to organize a way to encourage government courtesy and efficiency? After all, if we are looking to promote the idea that government is the place where a community takes action to solve problems, shouldn't we improve the product that we are trying to sell? Who will step forward to organize this?

That really should be done to prepare the ground for what could come next, which is a new engagement of citizens with issues of interest to them in their communities. We should begin in our high schools. During the years from 13 to 19, lifelong civic values are formed.

We should work with the popular history and civics teachers in our high schools to bring the issues of the day and the issues of the town into the classroom—not to propagandize but to openly invite students to learn, research, and offer advice to the community on a wide range of issues. This is where the hypnosis falls apart. This is where democracy finds its feet again.

This summer I asked America's independent and community radio stations to get involved with those same teachers in our high schools, to make students into community reporters and commentators. I reminded these independent news stations that they have the technology and the dramatic missions that young people crave. I said young people will never become robots if they are enlisted in the cause of truth at an early age.

What we do in schools, we must also do in colleges and then in the general community. But if we only have the means to focus on the high schools, that will be enough. These young people will be voting in only a few years. If we support their increased civic engagement as they move through college and into the community, we will have raised an army of citizens immunized against corporate hypnosis. Our victories for needed reforms will come naturally. With an engaged and informed citizenry, who knows what good we might do, and what great civilization we might yet again move toward? The crashing climate will organize young people soon, but we can and should advance the schedule.

I urge you to think young, to link with moderates on the other side of the fence, and to approach the schools and teachers who can help you connect young, rising citizens to the issues that will shape their lives.

If you believe that human beings, in addition to all their other instincts, want to help create and live in a happy, sustainable, just, creative and cooperative world, then you must believe that people are to be trusted in their politics, so long as they are encouraged to study everyone's experience and study the competing points of view—and so long as they are raised with enough love and security to be capable of empathy. We need not force a liberal agenda on our society, any more than we need force our political opinions on our children. We can enjoy life instead of banging our heads against the old walls. If we encourage an awakened thoughtfulness, democracy and justice will have all the victories our hearts can handle.

We should never let up in our efforts to protect young children from poverty and other abuses. We should support young parents so they will raise their children well. This is not only the right thing to do, and therefore the proper goal of political action, but we must understand that one of the credible theories of the divide between the political left and the right is that those on the right have a deeply-seated belief that people are basically selfish and bad and in need of authority figures who will straighten them out. Those on the left have more of an innate trust in the good of people, and they therefore look to remove the stresses and abuses that would corrode that naturally gregarious and cooperative sense of sharing and goodness—empathy, to put it in a word. And what makes a child fear others, distrust others, have a bad opinion of people in general? It is a rough childhood where the security children need has been stripped away by a culture that overstresses the parents. So, let us care about how children are raised, for it determines whom they become.

I began this talk with a view of the corporate takeover artists who shaped our present world. To reshape it now will take a new kind of takeover artist, whose guiding value is not greed but love. It will take artfulness, strategy, energy and resources to do what now needs doing.

Thank you very much.

What We are *For*

Ms. Haddock speaking in Keene, New Hampshire, April 5, 2003

Thank you very much. In 1997, I read an op-ed in the Boston Globe that described how, in the middle of the night, two members of the House of Representatives added an amendment to a bill, giving $50 million as a subsidy to a tobacco company. When I started asking how that could happen, I was told to study campaign finance reform. Big money donations are the cause of such mischief, I was told.

Indeed, a candidate or politician today has to sell his or her soul to the special interests in order to get the tremendous sums necessary to fund an election and reelection—or else be a millionaire.

Giving money to a candidate cannot help but translate to access. It is a natural thing, even though it is wrong. It is wrong because the public official who provides special access to his or her campaign donors is stealing that access away from the citizens of the state or district to whom it rightfully belongs. But as long as there are large political donations, there will be that sale of stolen goods.

The wealthy interests who fund the campaigns of our public officials get a great deal back in the form of subsidies, tax breaks, environmental deregulation, worker safety deregulation and more. It comes to over $150 billion each year, counting conservatively. Certainly, that figure does not take into account the true cost of poisoning all our streams with lead and mercury and blowing up the Appalachian Mountains for easy coal and, in in the process, burying so many freshwater streams. It does not take into account the cost to the globe of climate change, but the politicians who take industry money then turn their backs on alternative energy development, close their eyes to oil wars and all the rest. The real cost of this corruption is uncountable; it is not possible to count the cost of a lost world and a lost democracy, is it?

When I was young our politics was largely financed by our friends. Maybe the drugstore owner or the mill owner wrote some bigger checks than ours, but the scale of things was still local and human. Corporations were not allowed to write those checks, because, financially, they dwarfed the people.

In my parent's time, Teddy Roosevelt had valiantly worked to outlaw the participation of corporations in politics. But the laws passed during his administration were whittled away over the years since. The McCain-Feingold Bipartisan Campaign Finance Reform Bill, which I walked across the U.S. for and which passed last year, puts some of the old wall back up to keep corporations out of politics. But big money still rules our politics, so we have a lot of work remaining to fix this problem. It is, after all, the mother of all political problems in the U.S. and in many other nations that, like us, falsely claim to be healthy democracies. A democracy is a land where average people can defend their rights to a decent life. It isn't happening here, friends, but we'll fight to get it back.

One of our weapons will be the public financing of our elections

Here is how public financing works: First, it's voluntary, so there are no constitutional problems about limiting anyone's rights. The candidate who wants to participate has to personally collect a certain number of qualifying signatures and small contributions—usually in the five-dollar range—from registered voters in their district. This demonstrates community support for the candidate. Anyone who has been active in a parent-teacher group or scouting or some other such thing will have an easy time of it. Someone who has not helped in their community will find it harder sledding.

When the candidate meets these requirements, the campaign receives advertising money from the state elections fund. The candidate must agree to neither raise nor spend any other money, including his or her own. That neatly gets special interest contributors and billionaires out of the picture. The cost of such a system is about a tenth the cost of paying off special interest contributors with tax breaks and other favors that later come at the expense of every taxpayer.

I truly hope I can help get this clean money reform enacted in the states and at the federal level. To have helped in some small way is the legacy that I wish to leave to my 16 great grandchildren. And, in the bigger picture, this is the least we owe to those living and dead who fought for our democracy.

We Americans have a dream of independence, of responsible self-governance and of individual freedom. We want to see our country as a beacon in the world for the great human dreams of freedom and justice, and simple kindness and common sense. We have enshrined our Declaration of Independence and our Bill of Rights with great pride, for they are the roadmaps to the pursuit of happiness.

We hold to this dream in spite of the reality of our history. We have engaged in slavery and we have wiped out noble races who lived here first. We hold to our dreams in spite of everything, because it is our duty to hold to this dream, imperfect as we have been in hewing to it. All the nations of the world remind us of our duty when they send us their children to educate or to assimilate into a culture where individuals have a chance to freely live up to their unique potentials. The French reminded us of our duty with their gift of Lady Liberty, standing yet in New York Harbor. Oh, I hope they do not take her back!

Now let me turn to the news of the day—our nation's recent and preposterous attack on Iraq—though our own inspectors told us there are no weapons of mass destruction being built there.

In our slow and wobbly path forward to a better world, we do sometimes find ourselves making a great step backward. That is happening now, as we discard our Bill of Rights and discard international cooperation and are all for naked self-interest instead of justice. It has happened before. We have invaded and bombed before, when we might have negotiated, or when we might have worked cooperatively.

So, what do we do if we are at war because our elected representatives are representing oil interests and defense contractors and not the will and interests of the people? Well, we have gone to jail before and suffered popular abuse before. People among us have done that, standing against great wrongs, holding the torch of democracy in dangerous times. It is that way now, as many prepare to go to jail rather than pretend that nothing serious is happening in America. Can our shaky old hands hold that great torch? Well, we must all do our best until the nation awakes again and rightly embraces her dream again.

It is a shared dream, and we stand here together today because we care about each other. We care about our brothers and sisters who struggle in poverty and injustice, not only here but everywhere in the world.

Yes, we are for freedom. We are for the justice that allows all people the proper pursuit of happiness. We are for the elimination of poverty. We are for equal rights. We are for the protection of our fragile environment. We are for the education of our children. We are for treating the ill, and we are for housing all the people. We are for jobs and decent livings. That is all to say that we are for love. We are for love. And most of all and forever, while others are for bombs and death and lies, we are for love and the truth. Thank you.

After a 2003 peace protest in Union Square, New York City

Trust Your Own Values

> *Ms. Haddock speaking to the Freshmen Class at Franklin Pierce College, New Hampshire, Friday, September 5, 2003; her memoir was required reading for the incoming freshmen:*

Thank you. It is a great pleasure to grow old and to be asked to dispense advice and to not have to follow it oneself. In that department, let me urge you to go to bed early, get up at dawn, keep well ahead of your studies, stay well behind your credit limit, refrain from smoking and drinking and wild living. I give you that advice, not because I have ever followed all of it myself, but because life's pleasures are all the more delicious if an old lady has told you to do otherwise.

The fact is, life is a feast of great pleasures and we are rude to our Creator if we do not partake of the beauty and fun and pleasure of this life. So, I do hope you will take care of yourself and that you will mind your schedules to the extent that you will not always be behind and worried and stressed and missing out on the joy all around you. The captain of a well-run ship can afford the time to enjoy the breeze and the view. Be that to your own life, starting now with college. It is a challenge, I know, but if you keep at it, you will get the hang of living well in this life.

You will see that some of the students around you are forever behind and worried, and others seem on top of it and have a smile. Your choice, indeed. The moment of truth is when you are tempted away from your resolve. Will you be a person of strong character? Here is the test of it: a person of character stays true to a resolution long after the mood has passed in which that resolution was made. Watch for that: Your conscious overview of your daily life can guide you toward improvements that will strengthen your hold on life and its happiness. Let me warn you more specifically that problems like depression and chronic procrastination are always a good excuse for a visit to the health center where you can get very useful help. The brain is no less fixable an organ than the stomach, and we do get our aches and pains and should go for help sooner rather than later. And be advised: if you come to a point sometimes when you cannot imagine your life working out, cannot imagine getting to a happy future, you are depressed; what you are feeling is not real, and you should go talk it out with a pro.

Now, that is all boilerplate advice. Let me tell you something more interesting. You come into college with the expectation of learning many new things—of becoming an expert in many areas. But there is one area where you are already the expert, and where the professors and the other old birds are not. Young people bring something special and, if you are not fully aware of this superior quality, you might waste it unknowingly.

I am not speaking of your athletic or more personal areas of strength and stamina, though I am sure you are very impressive to watch in action. I am speaking of your view of the world, which in many ways is superior to the view seen by older eyes.

Trust your sensibilities toward justice and fairness and toward the environment and peace. Understand that your value judgments in these areas are better because they have not been beaten down or crusted over. Information overload can make us insensitive. While your eyes are yet wide open—and also your heart—trust what you see. Do not hang back from involvement in addressing the problems of the world, waiting to become an expert. You are expert enough. You are our annual resupply of new eyes and fresh hearts to give our sorry species its best hope for improvement and survival. Take your part in the great dramas and the great struggles now still in their opening acts in this world. It is the part where you storm on stage with a confused but mischievous look and the audience cheers you madly. Don't wait to know the part too well, or the moment will pass.

What is your passion? The right place for you is directed by that passion. Or are you drifting, looking for your passion? Let your curiosity lead you to it. Trust the force of that curiosity. Be brave when your curiosity takes you to places you would rather not go—it knows what it is doing, and it has served you well for much longer than you can possibly imagine.

Look around every now and then and wonder what all this life is about. Whom is served by all this life? Whom does life serve? Life serves life, and we are happiest and at our best when we let our full life force—indeed our divine life force—rise within us as we engage our lives in service to the world—to the life around us. We are happiest when we are serving life and adding to its health and bounty. We are simply made that way—made for cooperation and togetherness of every kind.

This is an extraordinary time you have happened to come. What an amazing world! The young woman college student in Iran, wearing her Levis under her burka, is your sister and your friend. The farmer in Central America who is trying to get a fair price for his coffee beans so that he can build a better house for his children is your uncle and a man you deeply respect. The Navajo woman who is fighting for the right to stay on land that has been her family's for generations is your grandmother, and she needs your help.

It is not too much at all. It is all quite beautiful. Cast your heart into this world right now, for your eyes and your heart are open and your senses of justice and fairness and your sense of the right thing to do for the planet that sustains us is fully matured

and at its perfect moment to give hope and progress to the world. Don't save yourselves for later; spend yourselves today in love, and your investment will come back to you a hundredfold.

Most of the social progress of the past hundred years has come from students demanding a better world.

A good friend of mine was flying across the U.S. this past week and his seatmates were a young man and woman from Iran. The man was a naturalized U.S. citizen. The young woman had come here more recently. She told my friend how she had grown up under the artillery barrages of the Iran-Iraq War. She described how the Iranians saw that war: that the Americans had built up the Shaw's army to be among the strongest in the region, but that, when he was toppled by the Ayatollah, the U.S. then armed Saddam Hussein in Iraq and encouraged him to take down the Iranian army a few notches. It was in that game that she found herself as a child target of artillery. My friend asked her if she did not resent Americans for that time in her young life. She said that she tried not to hold Americans responsible for the actions of their government, as she hoped she wouldn't be held responsible for the actions of the Iranian government. She said that Americans seemed so kind and so unaware of what was being done in their names around the world, and she said she thought it must be like being the children in a family where the father is in the underworld—that their lives are comfortable, but they know something is wrong. She said that she did not like to tell Americans about all that she knew, because it was kind of a shame to wake them up to all this when their lives were so cluelessly blissful—her words.

Well, as citizens of a democratic republic, we are indeed responsible for what our nation does in our name, and it is no discourtesy to awaken us into the engaged citizens we must be.

America is a great country and we love it. We love this planet, too. And you young people here today are the bright eyes that must be the open and awake eyes, though still full of joy and honor, love and mischief, duty and courage to serve life in a time when life is challenged by its old foes: fear and hate and ignorance.

May you be a great brotherhood and sisterhood of love and action. Arrange your personal lives so that you have the time and resources to take your part on this great stage. And smile the smile of the peaceful warrior whose weapons are love and light, and ever more love and ever more light.

Thank you and good luck. If it ever gets too crazy, do come down to my porch in Dublin and we'll talk it over, if I'm not away on some adventure of my own. Do call first. Your dean has my number and is to give it to any who ask.

Thank you.

Back at Harvard

Ms. Haddock speaking at the John F. Kennedy Forum at Harvard's Kennedy School of Government, October 2, 2003. She began her campaign, Working Women Vote, with this speech in the school's atrium amphitheater. Students and professors watched from the seats around her and from the layered balconies above. She considered the speech a letter to the Supreme Court, as the Harvard podium would give her words additional heft. McConnell, the California Democratic Party and others had sued to overturn the new McCain-Feingold law. The Supreme Court, soon after this speech, upheld the law, though, several years later, in Citizens United, they reversed themselves.

Thank you. It is a great honor to be here at Harvard's Kennedy School of Government. I thank you for inviting me and for coming this evening to hear me.

I have spoken to Harvard students before, though the circumstances were quite different. Young men—for they were all men—of the Harvard Business School would come to their lunch and dinner, and a young girl in a booth at the door would ask to see their meal cards. It was 1927. Several of the students would bring me books to read, as I seemed intent on learning things. Oswald Spengler's "Decline of the West," which had come out in 1922 and was a pessimistic prediction of the despotism and worldwide warfare to come, was still what everyone was reading and discussing. So, I was constantly brought that book by young men, and I always said I was glad to finally have a copy to read.

The pay for my job was not much, but I saved it up and enrolled the next year at Emerson, after working the summer as a maid at a Nantucket inn. I had a head start at Emerson thanks to all the books the Harvard boys lent me when I worked here.

I am deeply honored to be speaking from the podium where last week a true hero of democracy spoke to you—Polish president Lech Walesa. I wish I could have been here for that, although I do know some of what he said: In speaking of the Polish shipyards in the 1970s and 80s, he said, "there are special places where you can feel the future."

Quite so! There are places and times when the future of the world seems hanging like a chad, waiting for one butterfly's wings to move the world this way or that. We are poised on such a moment, and I think most of you can feel it—can feel the future. The world is waiting to go this way or that, and our individual efforts in the next year are those butterfly wings. Our glaciers are melting; our democracies and our basic human rights are poised for advancement or destruction; our American economy and our role in the world—so many things—are now poised to go this way or that. It is almost too much to contemplate, too much to worry about. We can feel the future, though we don't yet know which future it will be.

So much of my own energy lately has been devoted to campaign finance reform. The bill that we finally got through Congress is now waiting for the Supreme Court's decision. Like so much else, it is poised on a delicate balance. It will probably come down to one vote, and that may be the vote of Justice O'Connor once again. We can only pray for a good outcome.

The McCain-Feingold bill that became the law and is now before the Supreme Court does chase corporate money out of our federal elections, which is a good but imperfect accomplishment—if the Court will let us keep it. The very high political price paid for that victory was a doubling of the limit of personal money that can be donated to a campaign, increasing it to $2,000 per person, per election, with the primary and general election counted separately. That's a lot of money, and I suppose the most heartbreaking scenario would be if the Court struck down the prohibition on corporate money but left in the doubling of the personal money limit. We are praying for the Court's wisdom and lately that is a hard prayer.

The issue is this: Can we keep our democracy human-scaled, or is it to be a playing field only for financial giants? Have we, the people, lost our government? And if we have, what alternatives for action do we have that are worthy of our peaceful hearts?

If I were a lawyer and allowed to speak before that Court, I would have told them about so many people I met on my long walk who came to tears when they described their frustration at the loss of their America. "Beyond our control now," they said. "Bought right out from under us," they said. "All in the hands of fat cats and scoundrels"—that is what so many people said and do think, and they have much evidence to support their opinions.

The law that is now before the Supreme Court provides that corporations cannot finance federal candidates for office. It further provides that ads that look and smell like campaign ads, when run during a campaign, should be financed by individuals, not by corporations, and that those people should file disclosures like any other campaign committee.

No human being, acting individually or in a group, is deprived of speech by the new law. The law in fact allows the speech of the individual to again be heard. It is a modest patching-up of the old campaign laws, in that the first prohibition of corporate money in our elections was the good work of Republican Teddy Roosevelt.

Some of the Justices seem uninformed of the fact that American democracy is in crisis and that Congress has now acted only in response to that crisis, doing so quite modestly and begrudgingly. Indeed, listening to the Justices ask their questions during the oral presentations a few days ago, I pictured them with powdered wigs, monocles and snuff boxes—they might as well have been in the 18th Century and on another continent, as the "let them eat cake" comments were sadly numerous.

I don't think that a 93-year-old former shoe factory worker should know more about the situation than they do, but that was the sinking feeling that came over me as I listened to them. I wished that I could drag them by their frilly collars to the living rooms where real Americans shared with me their disgust for the—excuse me—whorehouse that Washington has become—tragically become, indeed, as so many of our sons and daughters have given life itself for our freedoms and, chief among them is our freedom to govern ourselves through the election of representatives who will represent us and not just the rich and not just the powerful, and who will be our champions against the corruptions of big banking, big medicine, big energy and all the rest.

If the new law's modest sandbags against a flood of corruption cannot be allowed by the Court, then we must rethink our country in fundamental ways, although that rethinking may be unsettling and dangerous. But here it is: The great masses cannot be left thinking that they are powerless under this system, or they will in their own way choose other systems. The people are the seat of power itself and they are not likely to stand by while the air they breathe and the water they drink and the milk of human kindness itself is poisoned by the greed of a powerful elite, and while their own ability to provide for themselves and their families and communities is eroded toward poverty and treadmill credit enslavement. No, the presumptions of the elite, unchecked by a government of the people, are spiraling toward a collapse, and if the Supreme Court Justices cannot stand apart from the elite long enough to see the emergency, then change will come in unregulated ways—or the ways of the demagogue—that must make us tremble.

While we work—and we must continue to work—to weaken the unfair influence of the rich and the powerful international elite in our elections, we must also look for ways to strengthen the ability of ordinary people to have a meaningful voice. I think we are seeing that in the Internet and its fundraising capacity. It is opening a new era in our politics, both in terms of communicating information and fundraising, and it looks a lot more like democracy than does the $2,000 a plate chicken dinner and the $200,000 corporate donation. I hope you all will give a little bit of money and other energy to your favorite candidates, and the Internet offers easy ways for you to do so. If we all give a little to the champions of our values, then a people-powered democracy—the only real kind of democracy—can have a fighting chance.

It is interesting that today's New York Times reports that China's president is calling for more democracy in China as an antidote to corruption. Large political systems have corruption. The opposite of corruption is democracy. People tend to not choose to be oppressed and exploited and starved when they have a voice in the matter. Look at the great tax giveaway to America's richest of the rich and please see it as a failure of representative democracy, which it is. See it as a profound crisis, which it is.

And to Sandra Day O'Connor, who gave us the Florida decision and all that came from it, here is your chance to square your account with heaven and history.

Now, isn't it too bad the public doesn't own the airwaves so we could really have some inexpensive campaigns? Wait—we do own our airwaves? We do issue cable franchises to our cities? Well, then, it is too bad that we don't act the proper part of the owner. Why should we pay through the nose for our own air during campaign season?

Because so many new forces are in play, I will not be overly discouraged if the imperfect campaign reform bill is rendered even more imperfect by our imperfect Supreme Court. I will not call them by the names I may be thinking. Indeed, if human-scaled politics is to prosper, it requires a civil tone, and we are surely in control of what we say, and it does take the cooperation of both sides to have a shouting match. I do not mean that talking nicely will stop the rise of fascism, but I do mean that we can fight with the words and values of our higher civic sensibilities, even as we do battle.

The harsh divide between the political right and left, and indeed between the political right and the old middle, is now becoming dangerous. Points of view, often fueled by misinformation, unthinking xenophobia and racism, are pushing us into a time of domestic as well as international confrontation. The far right now equates honorable dissent with treason and terrorism. The angry voices on talk radio and in the newspapers and websites do not fully understand what they do. They do not grasp what happens when civil temperaments and good humor and respected differences of opinion are eroded by the acid of insult, interruption and shout, and when, little by little, the lower potentials of human nature are let off their leashes and instances of violence begin to rise, as they have done at other times and places in the history of our species…

All of us must exert ourselves in the coming months. America and the world will be dramatically influenced by the coming election.

This is a special place; this is a special time in America when we can feel the future. It is frightening, but it is exciting. It is your future more than mine. I wish you luck, and I ask you to wish me luck and lend a hand where you can. Thank you and goodbye.

In the spring of 2003 Doris
Haddock launched a voter registration drive in the swing states. She traveled through nearly all the states east of the Mississippi, taking over the jobs of working women long enough for them to register to vote. The jobs included a mermaid at a water park, an alligator feeder at a roadside alligator park, a bartender in New Orleans and many others. The events were designed to attract news coverage that would make the point that working women needed time off to register and vote. Indeed, the events were sometimes attended by voter registration officials who made adjustments to their programs.

She organized these and other voter registration events from Key West to Duluth. She went door-to-door in housing projects, including Chicago's notorious Cabrini Green, and found a warm welcome everywhere without exception.

She went home to New Hampshire to rest before beginning the western states, but something then happened: New Hampshire's Democratic candidate for the U.S. Senate left the race just a few months before the election, leaving the Republican incumbent without an opponent. She called the state party and asked if she might step into the ring, just to keep the incumbent pinned down at home (he was otherwise an effective surrogate for President Bush) and continue her work to educate people about campaign finance reform.

The party said yes. At age 94, Mrs. Haddock was a candidate for the United States Senate.

Feeding a storm of alligators while Jamie registers to vote and Orlando TV stations and newspapers report.

One of Ms. Haddock's many "Working Women Vote" events

Ms. Haddock walked through cities on her voter registration drive, but travelled between cities in a small RV painted for the occasion by artist friend Julie Broxton

Registering voters in the Little Haiti and Overtown communities of Miami

Planning the world's first underwater voter registration of professional mermaids at Weeki Wachee Springs, near Tampa

Let's Talk About You

After voter registration events throughout Pennsylvania and West Virginia, Doris "Granny D" Haddock spoke at Marshall University, Huntington, West Virginia, on Tuesday, November 4, 2003 (excerpt):

New creative leaders must take the stage and be willing to look squarely at today's troubles and see past them to a better world. The creative leader sees possibilities unseen by others. But be sure the creative leaders you embrace lead from love and not fear; freedom and not cruelty and oppression. History has seen both kinds, rising from times of trouble.

And don't be afraid to be a leader yourself. We can all do it on the issues of our passions. For example, I have asked many to help me, and I will now ask you to help me, too. I will ask you—I do ask you now—to sign up to help register people at our voter registration tables.

That's all leadership is. It's asking for help.

You will not be alone if you help me; hundreds of people and small organizations have signed up to help us, and we are enough to change history, in our way.

I am an old Democrat. I don't care if you are a young Democrat or a young Republican, or a Green or an independent or if you are an anarchist because you like to be so bad and you look so good in black.

I don't care what you believe, so long as it is a belief in the future and in a better world. For this life is about service to each other. It matters little what you do or how successful you are, or what your old sins or crimes or shortcomings might be. If you give your life to the service of others, that is love and it is redemptive and joyful and will make your life and your soul complete.

And I am saying that this is not an ordinary moment in the history of the planet. It is a glorious time of trouble, a time of change and challenge, and the forces of heaven look upon us now and say, well, what are you going to do, little ones? Do you, as Americans, have the courage of your Constitution? Are you prepared to help lead the world to happiness, or to ruin? And which of you will lead, and who will follow? And which of you will be but the furniture of this age, the hapless consumers, the glaze-eyed and hypnotized, and who will be awake and brave? Who will say, I am for love in the world?

Will you ask me to help you, to follow you? I will, you know. Just ask for my help.

For I happen to know your secret—that you are the center of the world, that your actions ripple out and change everything, that your life is not only important to the world, but critical to it. I believe in you and in the biography that you are beginning to write in the world. I am reading your book right now and it has a wonderful beginning.

And all I ask of you, so that we may be brothers and sisters in the work of our hearts, is that you will vote and help others to vote. That is the baseline, the beginning point of our citizenship as Americans.

We are blessed to be Americans. But this blessing came by way of blood and hard work, and we must respect the sacrifices made for us and for our freedoms by finding our own voices, taking our own stands, and, damn it, by voting! Thank you!

With filmmaker Rebecca MacNeice in Asheville NC

Marching to the tunes of Tattoo in Milford, NH

Ms. Haddock accepted no PAC money in her campaign. Volunteers, including expert advisors on health, defense and the economy, arrived from Harvard and other universities and from D.C., pitching tents in the woods across the stream from her forest home. While she lost, as expected (Judd Gregg, her opponent was the nation's most popular U.S. Senator in his home state), she brought in a bit more than a third of the vote, twice what pundits had predicted. She carried Portsmouth and some other communities. More important, she pinned Gregg down, and her campaign recruited enough new voters, both old and young, to help swing New Hampshire into the blue for the presidential race. That was her main hope in running, which allowed her election night party to be a victory celebration.

Her televised debate with Sen. Gregg won her the audience poll. A high moment in that debate was when Gregg, whose flood of television ads featured him fly fishing in a stream, challenged her criticism of his environmental votes. "I have seen your television ads, Senator," she replied instantly, "and I hope you did not drink that water you were standing in…" She went on to knowledgably report on the toxicity of New Hampshire water, mostly from pollution coming from as far away as Ohio Valley coal plants—a crisis furthered by his votes in the Senate. Her campaign used walks across the state to educate voters on the need for campaign finance reform and argue against a second term for President Bush.

The following is Ms. Haddock's formal announcement to run for the U.S. Senate, made in the lobby of the New Hampshire State House, Concord, Thursday, June 17, 2004. It was rated by the head of the political science department of a New Hampshire university as "the best announcement speech in American politics this year and perhaps any other."

I Walked—Now I'll Run

Thank you. My name is Doris Haddock and I am a candidate for the U.S. Senate from New Hampshire. While I am happy to step forward in the absence of other Democrats, I certainly do not do so as a sacrificial lamb. I am running to win. I am a realist, of course, but I am not a defeatist.

For those who may be concerned about my age, let me say that I have outlived most of the things that can kill me, and am good for another election or two. Nevertheless, I make my pledge right now to stick to one term, and I have the biological ability to follow through with that pledge, while Mr. Gregg, who, two elections ago, made a pledge to not run for a third term, has neither the ripe age nor, it seems, the willpower to deliver on his promise.

For those who may doubt my capacity to serve, let me assure them that, while I may struggle for the right word from time to time, I can yet string my words together somewhat better than even our current president. And, while I need glasses for some reading, I can see clearly the difference between a necessary war and an unnecessary war, and the difference between a balanced budget and a deficit. Most importantly, I can read the Constitution and its Bill of Rights very easily and clearly, and, when elected, I will do what so many others in today's Washington have not had the decency to do, which is to abide by their oath to defend it.

I am running for the U.S. Senate against a good man, Judd Gregg, who has allowed himself to become an enabler of George Bush and his neocon scourge now afflicting our nation and the world. I, Doris Haddock, am running so that our voters might at the very least send Mr. Gregg a message that we expect our senators to represent common sense and the interests of our country and of our working people and children, even when to do so requires the courage to go against one's party.

And I am running to do a favor for my many Republican friends who are most uncomfortable with how far their once-venerable party has strayed—once a bastion of sensible federal spending and small business defense. I am the angry grandmother of the New Hampshire family, come off my porch to ask young Judd what in the world he is thinking when he supports Bush's military misadventures, supports the transfer of billions of our tax dollars to billionaires, and supports the shipping of our jobs overseas with tax breaks that actually encourage this tragic loss. New Hampshire has financial problems because the tax dollars we pay—and we pay plenty—are being wasted in Washington instead of returned to our people, our schools, and our real security needs. Mr. Gregg, I am not running to give you a scare; I am running to win, because I think almost anyone could do a better job representing our American values and our New Hampshire needs, and I am indeed almost anyone.

Mr. Gregg is a good and likeable fellow, rather like a charming but troubled son-in-law. We do like the fellow, but we shake our heads at what he has done to the precious treasure we have entrusted to him.

How might I, in the U.S. Senate, serve New Hampshire—my birthplace and always my home?

We the people need a peace-loving government that protects us and our values by promoting peace and justice in the world. Terrorism is the twisted child of poverty and injustice, and  we cannot buy our way or arm our way around that fact. We cannot support cruel dictators and expect otherwise. We must become energy independent so that we are free to pursue justice and not self-interest in the world's affairs. I will work for that. I applaud Mr. Gregg when he stands up for energy independence and for the environment, but I pledge to do more, and to move America toward responsible stewardship of our resources for our children's children, and for their children's children, which is the only true conservatism.

We the people need well-funded education for our children and the best health care for each other. School funding—a crisis not only in New Hampshire but in nearly every state—can be much relieved if we can get back more of the federal tax dollars we pay. And if Mr. Gregg would not enable the neocons to transfer so many billions to the billionaires, we could do so. If Mr. Gregg would work for more justice instead of more bombs, again we could do so, and pay for all the health care we need. I will vote to bring the resources back to the people who need them, who in fact provide them by their hard work and sufficient federal tax payments.

The largest con of the 20th and 21st Centuries is the globalization of the workforce. We need to encourage the localization, not globalization, of the economy—and thereby strengthen it and humanize it. Our political leaders have failed us monstrously in this matter, as more and more of our jobs, and more and more members our middle class, have been sold down the ocean. Mr. Gregg, though he is a fine-looking man and a good New Hampshirite, should be ashamed of his role in this ongoing destruction of America's economic base—a loss to every family.

Look at our beautiful state—its waters, its air, its great forests and mountains—and, oh, its people! We do not need much to live well here. We need to be left alone in most matters. We need to join together in other matters, where joint action can create great resources for our children and each other. We of this Granite State are blessed with common sense and deep community. I should be most honored to represent these things of ours in Washington and let them see what flint we are made of when they try to take away our peace, our justice and our common treasure.

But it is not enough to elect our representatives so that they might stop bad things from happening. They must have a vision for the future of their people. That should be what every campaign is about. It shall certainly be so with mine. Thank you.

The Five Nations

During her 2004 U.S. Senate campaign, Ms. Haddock spoke at a Fourth of July town picnic at the History Center of Portsmouth.

Thank you. I am honored to speak to you on this special day of the American year.

We tend to think that our form of government began with Tom Jefferson and friends, but they were only extending a tradition of democracy that existed on this soil for centuries before they came.

When our founders—and very specifically Constitutional Convention member John Rutledge of South Carolina and his Committee of Detail—were struggling with the form of the new U.S. Constitution, they carefully studied the constitution of the Iroquois League of Nations, taking it as their model. That great Native American constitution, which originated somewhere in the 14th to 16th Centuries, was well known to the early Anglo settlers, who wrote it down for the first time, just as the Native Americans recited it to them. In a moment, I shall read from it.

The animal symbol of the Five Nations of the Iroquois was the eagle, like ours, perched high with its eye looking out for any danger to the peace.

Another important symbol of the Five Nations was the cluster of five arrows. Look at our dollar bill and you will see our newer cluster of thirteen arrows in the iron grip of the eagle. The Iroquois Constitution says this: "As the five arrows are strongly bound, this shall symbolize the complete union of the nations. Thus, are the Five Nations united completely and enfolded together, united into one head, one body and one mind. Therefore, they shall labor, legislate and council together for the interest of future generations."

Well, that would be us. They, too, are our forefathers. And in times of trouble we should take their council.

They had wise laws. While the men had all the power in council, the women had the power to choose the men who would lead—a workable balance, for their day—more about the women's power in a moment.

The men and the women had their own, highly

democratic council fires, where concerns could be voiced and presented for action to the nation.

They had quite an elegant disarmament policy, which went like this:

"We now uproot the tallest pine tree and into the cavity made thereby we cast all weapons of war. Into the depths of the earth, down into the deep under-earth currents of water flowing to unknown regions we cast all the weapons of strife. We bury them from sight, and we plant again the tree. Thus, shall the Great Peace be established."

They had two houses of legislative deliberation, plus an executive and judicial branch, more or less, and veto powers, impeachment, and a fair justice system that respected the dignity of every person. We should not admire that history as outsiders; we should embrace it proudly as a part of our own history, ever working to mend the historical divisions that might keep us from accepting its wisdom and humanity.

We would do well to install our new senators and representatives in the same way that we Americans did when we were the Five Nations. Here is a part of the ceremony, addressed to any new representative arriving at council:

"Your heart shall be filled with peace and good will and your mind filled with a yearning for the welfare of the people. With endless patience you shall carry out your duty, and your firmness shall be tempered with tenderness for your people. Neither anger nor fury shall find lodgment in your mind and all your words and actions shall be marked with calm deliberation. In all of your deliberations in Council, and in your efforts at law making, in all your official acts, self-interest shall be cast into oblivion."

In all your official acts, self-interest shall be cast into oblivion.

There is the model we still hold in our hearts for our democracy, isn't it?

Here is how, in their constitution, the Iroquois instructed their leaders to begin their great meetings:

"Offer thanks to the earth where men dwell, to the streams of water, the pools, the springs and the lakes, to the corn and the fruits, to the medicinal herbs and trees, to the forest trees for their usefulness, to the animals that serve as food and give their pelts for clothing, to the great winds and the lesser winds, to the Thunderers, to the Sun, the mighty warrior, to the moon, to the messengers of the Creator who reveal His wishes, and to the Great Creator Who dwells in the heavens above, Who gives all the things useful to men, and Who is the source and the ruler of health and life."

There are many beautiful passages in this first American constitution. It lays down specific rituals to keep the peace: For example: "If any man or any nation outside the Five Nations shall obey the laws of the Great Peace and make known their disposition to the Lords of the Confederacy, they may trace the Roots to the Tree and if their minds are clean and they are obedient and promise to obey the wishes of the Confederate Council, they shall be welcomed…"

I like some of the specifics, rather reminiscent of the Old Testament. For example:

"When the Lords are assembled, the Council Fire shall be kindled, but not with chestnut wood."

We in New Hampshire might understand that, as chestnut wood sparks too much, and they wanted a peaceful meeting, without their robes catching fire.

If you want to know how the U.S. Constitution provides for a bicameral congress and the separation of powers, listen to this:

"In all cases the procedure must be as follows: when the Mohawk and Seneca Lords have unanimously agreed upon a question, they shall report their decision to the Cayuga and Oneida Lords who shall deliberate upon the question and report a unanimous decision to the Mohawk Lords. The Mohawk Lords will then report the standing of the case to the Firekeepers, who shall render a decision as they see fit in case of a disagreement by the two bodies or confirm the decisions of the two bodies if they are identical. The Fire Keepers shall then report their decision to the Mohawk Lords who shall announce it to the open council. If through any misunderstanding or obstinacy on the part of the Fire Keepers, they render a decision at variance with that of the Two Sides, the Two Sides shall reconsider the matter and if their decisions are jointly the same as before they shall report to the Fire Keepers who are then compelled to confirm their joint decision."

So, the Mohawk and Senecas were what we call the House; the Cayuga and Oneidas were what we call the Senate, and the Firekeepers were the conference committee or sometimes the Supreme Court, more or less.

As for fairness, listen to this:

"When the Council of the Five Nation Lords shall convene they shall appoint a speaker for the day. He shall be a Lord of either the Mohawk, Onondaga or Seneca Nation. The next day the Council shall appoint another speaker, but the first speaker may be reappointed if there is no objection, but a speaker's term shall not be regarded more than for the day."

They had a special take on women's rights:

"If any Confederate Lord neglects or refuses to attend the Confederate Council, the other Lords of the Nation of which he is a member shall require their War Chief to request the female sponsors of the Lord so guilty of defection to demand his attendance of the Council. If he refuses, the women holding the title shall immediately select another candidate for the title. No Lord shall be asked more than once to attend the Confederate Council. If at any time it shall be manifest that a Confederate Lord has not in mind the welfare of the people or disobeys the rules of this Great Law, the men or women of the Confederacy, or both jointly, shall come to the Council and upbraid the erring Lord through his War Chief.

"If the complaint of the people through the War Chief is not heeded the first time it shall be uttered again and then if no attention is given a third complaint and warning shall be given. When the Lord is deposed the women shall notify the Confederate Lords through their War Chief, and the Confederate Lords shall sanction the act. The women will then select another of their sons as a candidate and the Lords shall elect him. Then shall the chosen one be installed by the Installation Ceremony."

So, you see, the men were in charge only for so long as they behaved and served the people well and showed up for work. But if they are really troublesome, there is a remedy. Pay attention, Mitch McConnell:

"Should it happen that the Lords refuse to heed the third warning, then two courses are open: either the men may decide in their council to depose the Lords or to club them to death with war clubs."

Now, how did the Five Nations deal with housing, homelessness, the distribution of wealth? Quote:

"The soil of the earth from one end of the land to the other is the property of the people who inhabit it. The Great Creator has made us of the one blood and of the same soil he made us, and as only different tongues constitute different nations he established different hunting grounds and territories and made boundary lines between them.

When any alien nation or individual is admitted into the Five Nations the admission shall be understood only to be a temporary one. Should the person or nation create loss, do wrong or cause suffering of any kind to endanger the peace of the Confederacy, the Confederate Lords shall order one of their war chiefs to reprimand him or them and if a similar offence is again committed the offending party or parties shall be expelled from the territory of the Five United Nations. When a member of an alien nation comes to the territory of the Five Nations and seeks refuge and permanent residence, the Lords of the Nation to which he comes shall extend hospitality and make him a member of the nation. Then shall he be accorded equal rights and privileges."

So, you see, America's first immigration policy was quite humane, as it should be.

Now, as in the Old Testament, there are some sections that are less than generous, but overall you can see that the American sprit we embrace, enjoy and celebrate is more Native American than European. Isn't that a remarkable fact, hidden so long by the shame of our genocide against them and our education system that neglects our own history?

They did go to war from time to time, but, unlike our modern arrangement, the people had a say. Listen to it:

"Whenever an especially important matter or a great emergency is presented before the Confederate Council and the nature of the matter affects the entire body of the Five Nations, threatening their utter ruin, then the Lords of the Confederacy must submit the matter to the decision of their people."

It is a long document, and I have only read a small part of it for you, so that you can get its flavor and wisdom. We are people in a land of free people—people who have served each other with dignity and sacrifice for many centuries, going back long before the European invasion. On this Fourth of July, let us thank our Native American forefathers for what they have given us. Thank you.

In Faneuil Hall

Though Ms. Haddock was the New Hampshire Democratic Party's U.S. Senate candidate, the party failed to invite her to the Democratic National Convention in Boston. Her candidacy was never mentioned from the podium, nor was she—one of the finest orators of the new century—invited to speak. She therefore crashed the sessions and the parties, obtaining credentials from friends, speaking at side events, and gaining press that was well received at home. She also met political consultant Joe Trippi, the former campaign chairman of the Howard Dean campaign, at a bar near the convention hall. They hit it off, and Mr. Trippi made himself available on the phone and occasionally in person during her campaign.

Ms. Haddock speaking in Faneuil Hall, Boston, Tuesday, July 27, 2004 during the Democratic National Convention:

Thank you. Feel this place under you and around you. Know where you are. All the world knows the story of how the Americans became a free people, how they declared their independence, how they devised a constitution that is still an engine of fairness, of improvement, of justice and freedom. But the story seems remote sometimes. So, feel this place under you. Know where you are. Remember who we are.

This room, these walls, echoed the words of Sam Adams as he stood in this place and reminded Americans who they were and what they must do. In this very room we Americans heard George Washington and Daniel Webster shape the new Republic.

In this room William Lloyd Garrison helped define an American value system that could no longer admit of human slavery, and he defined nonviolent resistance in a way that was persuasive with Ruskin in England and Tolstoy in Russia and Gandhi in South Africa and India, and from Gandhi back to Martin Luther King in America—from this room.

And here spoke Susan B. Anthony to move our engine of equality forward again.

And here spoke John Kennedy and so many other Americans who loved freedom and justice and who pushed us to be a better people, moving ever along and up the Freedom Trail.

Feel this place. Remember who you are and why you are

here and understand that all of them and all of us are of one mind and sometimes are of one place. We are in this room. And perhaps those who have come before us are in this room yet, to see their work continue and be the real spirits of our inspiration.

Feel this neighborhood around you: The street corner of the Boston Massacre is but a few steps behind me; The Tea Party was but a few steps behind you. Revere's house, the Old North Church, are but across the way, still there, still living containers for our aspirations and our shared courage. Remember who we are and how we rise up when our liberty is threatened!

We are not a people to be trifled with, Mr. President. We are not to be trifled with, ye corporations who press down upon us like a plague of King Georges, turning our middle class into greeters and our lives into credit card indentures!

We shall have our lives in freedom, and we shall have our democracy as it was given us, made better by our own sacrifices.

We are here. Our revolution needs defending in this moment. We are come back to our room where we devise strategies and double our courage. We are in this room. We breathe its air. We hear its soft assent.

So. What is our plan? What shall we do?

We are having an election. As some will distrust the machinery of our voting, let us use mailed ballots—all of us who can.

Let us do nothing until the election except work on our campaigns and prepare people to vote.

After the election, let us repair our old ship of democracy with some new sails and masts, starting with the public funding of our elections and thereby the removal of special interest campaign donations. Maine and Arizona already have good programs, as you may know. Arizona's is under attack by a repeal put on the ballot by right wing interests. We must help Arizona keep its clean elections system. I will certainly go there.

In this state, Speaker Finneran cannot stand forever in the way of an improved democracy. Get him unelected and revive clean elections here. I know this is in the works.

And it is in the works in Iowa, and in West Virginia, and in Kentucky, North Carolina, Florida, Oregon and many other states. I have been there and seen the work, and these efforts merit your support.

And with or without the clean elections reform, we must end the double-dip pillage of public resources by broadcasters and cable systems, that get their airwaves and franchises from the public for a song, then charge their highest rates for election commercials. We need to require broadcasters to apply their lowest contract rates to election commercials, less fifty percent. This will reduce the leverage of fat cat donors.

Doing democracy ourselves is what it is all about. The Bill of Rights Defense Committees, now successful in over 300 towns and cities, are a model for us in moving many reforms that, in combination, will renew our revolution and return our politics to the human scale, where our freedoms and our futures can be protected.

We must work for other improvements, too, such as ranked-choice voting, where you can rank your favorite candidates and not risk splitting the vote.

And beyond the mechanics of campaigns and voting, we must understand that a nation can be free only so far as it is educated. Failing schools go hand in hand with the rise of oligarchy and worse. Underfunding of education is a conscious suppression of the citizens, and we must stop it and replace it with K-through-university funding for all who will choose it.

There are many things we can and must do.

If the president is defeated in November, this work will be easier. And the defense of our tax wealth and our environment and our Bill of Rights will be easier. If he is not defeated, our work will be harder, but we will do it anyway.

For, in this place, we remember who we are. We are the people of an imperfect union, the ordinary people of a great Republic still in the making, and, in that, we are no ordinary people at all. And it matters not if we arrived in the Ice Age or yesterday.

Indeed, if you are new to America, know that three-quarters of the freedom fighters of 1776 were born across the sea. Remember what America is: it is you the newcomer, as this is your place now. You have a voice here among equals. Know that you have a new duty to participate. The great word, by which we live and survive, is participation, because, as is said, democracy is not something we have, but something we do.

This is our place. This is our time to be in this room. And when we are gone, when we have all passed through this life, others will come to this room after us and remember what we did in our time for the American Republic. Thank you.

Reorganize the Democratic Party

Very early in the 2004 campaign, Ms. Haddock worried that the followers of Dennis Kucinich and the followers of Governor Howard Dean might not come together to work for the eventual nominee. She urged both men to begin planning for a merger of their supporters. She, in fact, hitchhiked in Florida to meet up with Mayor Kucinich at one point, urging him on the matter. He agreed to try (as did Mr. Trippi). When the Boston Democratic Convention was finally underway, Ms. Haddock spoke at a large meeting of the resulting Progressive Alliance; Thursday, July 29, 2004:

Thank you. There are so many things that I do not have to say to the people in this room. I do not have to go on and on about the danger our democracy faces right now. I do not have to lay out the case for the Bill of Rights or the environment or fair trade or world peace. I do not have to reason with you as to the case against torture or dictatorship. I do not have to speak to you about how we must not split our vote this year. I don't like preaching to the faithful, so let me tell you something you may not have thought about.

Our present emergency is upon us because our civic society has been dumbed-down by pared-down newsrooms, pared-down radio and television news, by dumbed-down schools, and by a corporate-run economic rat race that keeps people so busy trying to make ends meet that they have neither time nor energy left for the civic affairs of their town or nation.

You certainly know all this, and we celebrate the rise of independent media and the use of books and films to fill-in some of the gaps. But the gaps are awesome, and democracy cannot long survive when the people are not well informed with the truth, well interested, and well supplied with time and resources enough to participate.

But there is another thing that has been pared and dumbed-down over the past two or three generations, and that is the art of politics itself.

If the politics of a century ago can be likened to a banquet, the politics of today is like a fast food burger.

I am going to try to sell you on the idea of a richer politics, so let me tell you what it used to be like. Everybody used to be involved. You went to your Elks Club or your Women's Club, but you went to your party meetings, too. You worked your neighborhoods. You talked up your issues and candidates. It was a fairly constant thing, not just during the election season. Why? Because democracy is a lifestyle, not a fringe benefit of paying your taxes. Self-governance is a lot of work, but it's where you make your best friends and have your deepest satisfactions, after your family.

Just before I declared for the U.S. Senate last month, I was on a 23,000-mile road trip to register voters. There were many housing projects and low-income neighborhoods where the people had seen nobody dropping by to talk politics since the last election—or ever. The Democrats may come around, we were told, every few years to ask for their votes, but they weren't there

to listen to their problems or to help them craft political solutions. These people were of the opinion that, if the Democrats won or lost, their own lives wouldn't change much.

That is stripped-down politics. That is downright exploitive politics, when you come around begging for votes for your concerns, but you don't give a crouton in return. Oh yes, if your man or woman is elected, things will be better for everybody. But that is the top layer of the cake, but it does not trickle down, and in fact there is hardly any cake for the poor to eat. We have to put things right by being involved all year long, every year, and in every neighborhood that needs political help. That is movement building—not just stumping for candidates.

You will go to your home tonight, or to your hotel room, and you will turn on all the lights and have a nice hot shower, and watch television and not even think about the electrical power that makes it all happen. If you follow the electrical wires far enough away you will find West Virginia and Kentucky communities that are being ravaged without mercy by big coal companies, protected by corrupt politicians. The coal companies cut off the tops off whole mountain ranges, dump the rubble in their once-Eden-like valleys, and leave the mess to the people there. Every time it rains now, their homes flood. Giant pools of toxic sludge are everywhere, and when their dams break, toxins spill for miles. One recent spill in Inez, Kentucky, released more goo than the Exxon-Valdez, but this is the first you've heard of it.

Now, if you are worried if West Virginia and Kentucky go to the Republicans, you might first ask yourself this: Where the hell were you when they so needed your help? Where were you when residents of Cabrini Green in Chicago, or the slums of Ft. Myers or Miami or New Orleans or Los Angeles needed your organizing help and your voice added to theirs? They love their children as you love yours, and they only want decent lives. Do you think politics is just about raising money for candidates? Politics is about creatively serving the needs of your people, and the election is just the report card for how you are doing and how many people you have helped and how many people are following your leadership because you are always there for them.

So, don't let this new progressive alliance be another can of Betty Crocker icing for a cake that isn't there. Organize not just to win elections but to deserve to win elections.

If we can help people in distressed situations solve their problems, they will be there to speak out on the larger issues that concern many of the people in this room. But few people will speak up about global warming until they have a warm house for their own children. Building a national constituency for change requires that we first work together to solve a wide range of personal issues for people.

The new meetups that have become possible and popular this year are a powerful force for change, but only when they go further than being just a gathering of like-minded citizens; They must become organizing units for bringing in people who are not yet like-minded. They must become organizing units for people who will do more than sit around and share their feelings about politics; they must be platoons that go out and get real politics done, and that means helping people.

This is an amazing moment in all of our lives, and in the life of our great nation. Never has our democracy been so challenged, and never have so many patriots of every age risen up to take their part in its defense. In the last two years, never have I been less proud of my government or more proud of its people, including the whole lot of you in this room.

Thank you.

Why Facts Don't Matter to Our Opposition

The following speech, here abridged, was made by Ms. Haddock to a Quaker political action committee at Orchard House, home of the Alcotts, in Concord, Massachusetts on October 6, 2005:

We meet in a time when two great and growing divisions are separating us as Americans: rich versus poor and left versus right. I would like to speak to the second of these, as its resolution would help solve the other.

The political issues that divide the American people are great issues with severe consequences for the moral life of the nation and the fate of the planet. These are issues equal to the issues that divided us in 1860, and we should fear that.

In some ways the conflict of the Civil War was never resolved, but was rather accommodated, in the same way that smoldering coals under ashes are but a fire asked to bide its time. The sparks now swirl up fresh. The heat and danger we feel is the old conflict between those who believe that authority comes from above—from an Old Testament God, delivered through husbands, presidents, preachers, ayatollahs and plantation overseers to people arranged in layers according to their assigned worth. It is a conflict between those authoritarians and those others who instead believe that all men are created equal and that the authority to govern issues forth from them, upward to their government—our common vessel of community—and not downward. This is an element of the divide of 1860 and also of our own time.

Our differences are not locked into different economies of different regions, as was the case in 1860. Our differences are with our neighbors, our friends, our family members. We try now to argue this out peaceably across fences and dinner tables instead of across a bloodied continent, as before. But it is getting difficult to do so.

Today's conflict it is not only about the enduring unfairness between races, but also now a kind of involuntary servitude—one of the mind. It is the hardest kind to deal with, as the victims do not want to be emancipated. But they must be, if the suffering of this nation and of the world is to end.

Let us consider the self-repression of the political right. And in this argument, I am talking to some of my own friends and hoping they will open their minds to a new thought from me, for I offer it in good faith and friendship.

Where authority and power are believed to flow down from heaven to the White House and ayatollahs and husbands, then the free and joyful living of people stands in the way and can be quite the enemy of that organization chart. If you will remember the free spirit of those flower children who grew up in the 1960s, for example, you will also remember the harsh attitude that attended to their joys from the more traditional, often more rural, elements of our society, ending in gunfire at Kent State.

Those political leaders who rose from this time, who lived in this more open and freer way—less constrained by the rules of authority—were especially vilified by the clan of authority. You need only to think of the harsh treatment given to the Clintons, who were of this generation and climate, to know the truth of this. And it fits the international pattern, of course, that the woman, Ms. Clinton, would be singled out for the cruelest stones.

What attracted such hatred? It was their freedom, their sense of equality, and their joys.

And here it is: Those living under the clan of authority are not given the privilege—the natural right—of living their own lives. They do as they are told, say and think what they are told. Smothered is their curiosity and their healthy skepticism, and also their imagination, joy, freedom, and lust for life itself. When they see others actually living lives, they react with anger, as if someone had cut to the front of a line that, for them, never moves.

Those enthrall to authority, cowering under it, lose sight of their own lives. They will venerate above all else the symbol of the yet unruined potential of life: the curled-up unborn. The authority clan will have the image of an unborn baby as its flag, and they will claim to honor and defend innocent life, but that will be a great lie to themselves. For they will not be the ones to demand DNA testing of all prisoners on death row; they will not be the ones to demand health insurance for all children, or better nutrition in all schools, or peaceful alternatives to international conflicts. They will be the ones to rail against providing aid, for the authority clan parades itself as pro-life while it is a cult of death. Having died themselves, strangled by authority and fear, they cannot wish happy lives for others—they cling only to that magic symbol of what might have been. They relate to the unborn baby selfishly; it is themselves: unborn, still hoping for a life that remains unlived.

I am not talking about true political conservatives. People who follow leaders like Goldwater, Forbes, Will and Buckley do believe, in the great mainstream of American thought, that government is the council fire of community. They just want it not to be all consuming. But the people we are dealing with today, who are so far to the right of traditional conservatives that it is unfair to call them that at all, do not believe that our government is our council fire of community. They would replace it with a church, a strict family, and, as they have shown so many times in history, even with a dictatorship that derives from imagined divine or kingly powers, and with a reign of brutal authority that sanctions criminal aggressions on other nations, torture, and the suspension of civil liberties, the rule of law and the primacy of

truth. How many times have we seen this happen abroad, and how many times have we wondered if we would have the courage and the character to stand against it, if it happened here?

I think every man and woman of us wants to be a patriot of this great nation. How sad to miss your cue when the alarm bell rings! How horrible to be enslaved to the wrong way of thinking at such a time of national crisis! We owe it to our friends and neighbors to awaken them if we can, so they might stand with us.

I will propose a mental experiment to see if we can find some breadcrumbs to lead our friends out of this dangerous maze.

Imagine that your friend is very much pro-life and pro-war and doesn't see the conflict. I think you might notice that this friend of yours lives a slipcover-protected life and has not even allowed herself the freedoms of a good fantasy life. Let's repair that.

Let me suggest that we take her to a good arts district, rent her a studio apartment full of art supplies above a good sidewalk café, find her a lover and come back in ninety days to see if her politics have changed. As she lives a real life, as she explores her own potential, as she meets a rainbow of good people, she will learn to let others live and enjoy their lives, too. She will want to help the young woman artist next door who gets into trouble. She will begin to be amused and impressed, instead of angered and depressed, by the joyful, free-living people of this beautiful Earth.

When people begin to really live their lives, the black and

white certainties do not turn to shades of gray, but to the million-jeweled hews of the morning. That sparkle is the reality of life revealed. Life is about living, and about helping other real people get through this world with a minimum of pain and a maximum of human dignity. We simply can't do that with authoritarian politics and its deadly abstractions instead of real people. We can only do that with our love and our freedom to think for ourselves and act individually and as a community.

And that was the example of Jesus, wasn't it? Did He not challenge the organized church of His day, challenge its authority, and overturn its rules that had hardened into cruelties and corruptions? Did He not show us how we might act instead from the love and charity of our own hearts, and, in this rebellion, did He not say, follow Me? Are we not then, like Him, to think for ourselves? Is so grand a thing as the human mind meant to be wasted? Our founders were deeply spiritual and also deeply secular—a well-balanced condition of the mature mind that eludes today's political fundamentalists. Our founders respected human freedom and the urge toward greater equality. Over the centuries we have tried to make this nation a better expression of their intent, so that there would be no second-class citizens, no arbitrary authority that limited our life, liberty or pursuit of happiness. And the better angels of that Revolution do perch yet on our shoulders as we oppose the clan of authority, that cult of death, whose cloak of human oppression has cast its shadow over our children's future.

What must we do? We must bring the light of consciousness to people who are enslaved by the darkness. We must show them—make them see—the clear links between the Taliban and the American fundamentalists. It is about power, male power, and subservience.

The desperate attitude of the far right toward not only the unborn baby but even brain-dead people on life support reveals something about their true religion: they have little of it. There is nothing in their action that reveals a belief that life is eternal, that there is no death except as a doorway to something better. Their brand of Christianity simply does not relate to the teachings of Christ.

The worst of the hate-mongers who misuse the Bible to make million-dollar church incomes and push a political agenda of male domination and hate are easy to spot, for they cherry-pick Bible passages to suit their purposes. They disregard any turning of cheeks; they disregard the fact that Jesus never mentioned the homosexuality that they so fear. They seem not to fear that, as very rich men, they themselves might have a hard time driving their Hummers through the eye of the needle into heaven. They claim that every word of the Bible must be followed, but if they really believed that they would have stoned themselves to death years ago, as they are as sexually frisky and full of covetous looks as anybody else. They forgive themselves freely, of course.

They refuse a young girl an abortion for the same reason they would refuse her birth control: because in either case she would be exercising power and control over her own future—and such power and control is reserved for male authorities, below whom she is to cower and serve and reproduce. It is all about that, and we have to start saying so, so that the far right will no longer have women marching in its toxic ranks—at least the awakened ones.

If I ran the Democratic Party I would lay it all out in expensive advertising campaigns. I would have the sociologists and the psychologists talking about the tricks of mental slavery that are being used to trick decent Christians and other people into following un-Christian leaders and policies. As with any kind of mental counseling, progress depends on the spread of consciousness—of self-awareness. I would let more and more people come to understand the nature of the lies that surround them and defraud them. I believe they really are for life and for liberty, but they must be given better information, better moral and emotional guidance and support.

It is not easy. Imagine walking down a street in my Peterborough. You run across a retired couple and start talking politics. You somehow get on the subject of abortion.

"Listen," you say, "the Europeans have a very small percentage of the abortions we do in the United States. They have cut the number of abortions by providing better sex education, providing more contraception, and accepting a more open and honest attitude about the sexual lives of their young people. If your concern is to reduce abortions, surely you must become an advocate of these programs that actually do the trick!"

But the couple disagrees. They tell you "it isn't about doing what works in Europe and what might work here, it is about doing the right thing for the right reason and following the word of God."

Well, that was a real conversation I had in Peterborough, though I'm sure they must have been visitors.

If you wonder why the other side of the political aisle seems so resistant to the facts, it is because they are not interested in what works, what is pragmatic; they are interested in obedience to authority. It is nothing less than mental bondage to the cult of authority. This is of course unworkable in the civic arena, where pragmatism is the belief system we must share as our common ground. The only way to break through that problem is if our few national voices of authority will please give these authority-dependent people permission to think freshly about our important issues.

There is another way out of this dark maze, and that way is leadership. Better leaders can make great differences in the life of a society, but we cannot elect them if we do not change from electoral organizing to social organizing.

When I went on a 23,000-mile voter registration journey before the last election, I walked through many housing projects and low-income neighborhoods where no one from the outside had dropped by to talk politics since the last election. The Democrats only come around, I was told, every few years to ask for their votes, if even that, but they weren't there to listen to their problems, to help them craft political solutions, and to stand behind them and amplify their voices. These people were of the opinion that, if the Democrats won or lost, their own lives wouldn't really change much. These are millions of wasted Democratic votes. Millions.

It is simply exploitive politics to come around begging for votes without giving so much as a crouton in return. We have to be involved all year long, every year, and in every neighborhood that needs political help. That is movement building—not just stumping for votes.

The residents of Cabrini Green in Chicago, and the people of the slums of Ft. Myers, Miami, St. Louis and New Orleans told me they needed our organizing help and our voices added to theirs—for they love their children too and want decent lives. Many of the streets I walked in New Orleans were later strewn with the drowned poor, as if America had progressed no further than the days of the Titanic, when those traveling life in steerage are never offered the lifeboats. So much criticism has fallen on the president for the flooding disaster in New Orleans, but the Democrats have had a long century to make life better and they have not done so. The New Deal and other programs, offered at a distance, are helpful but no match for a party meetinghouse in every neighborhood to raise the political competency and expectations of the area.

In all these places, I gave out information and forms to help people who had been in prison to get their voting rights back. They had no idea. The Democratic Party never bothered.

So, politics is not just about raising money for candidates. It is not about trying to motivate people to register and to vote, if you have not motivated them to do so with your service to them. Politics is about creatively serving the needs of your people, and the election is just the report card on how you are doing and how many people you have helped and how many people know that their lives are changing because of what you are doing, in and out of office. They are following your leadership because you actually acted like a leader—you were there for them and they will follow you en masse to the voting booths.

We do get the government we merit or deserve, you see, and the crowd standing behind us in critical times is the crowd we have served through the years. They will also be there for the other issues that they otherwise might not work for. People will not speak up about the warm climate, I assure you, until they first have a warm bed for their own children. If you have helped them with that, they will follow you into new issues because they trust you and you have given them the extra time and resources to become involved. They are no longer living desperately, because of you.

And so, here are my two thoughts. We must help people see the mental traps that they are victim to, and we must do this by telling it like we see it, by asking them to see that the pro-life but pro-war movement is really a cult of death, that fundamental Christianity represents the opposite of Christ's teachings, that authoritarian control and elite profiteering are the strings of the far right's puppet show.

Let us indeed believe that all people are equal; but let us not assume that all political opinions are equal, for some are toxic and sociopathic and require our loving intervention. Let us intervene. Let us stand up in church gatherings; let us confront our friends; let us use the tools of mass communication to awaken people from the lies that bind them.

And let us return to real politics in the neighborhoods—especially those neighborhoods where we are most needed. As it stands now, people who do not receive the support they need from an ever-receding community are turning to the very mega-churches that have been politically killing those needed government services. This is a dangerous tailspin that we can only arrest with a political return to the neighborhoods. Let us demand of our party leaders that we move from electoral to social organizing, so that there is more rock and less hot air under our candidates as we move into the future.

We also must drain the swamps of anger that fuel the far

right. The true reason for that anger is a loss of power that has come with the rape of the middle class by big-box oligarchs and overlarge corporations, though a ventriloquist trick has been used to make it look like big government and the very liberals fighting for the people are the villains. We can only fix that by expanding the middle class and, in a million ways, giving people more power over their own futures. A candidate who promised to prevent banks or insurance companies from answering their telephones with computers would win any election. There must be so many ways to return a sense of power and respect to people, and all that will improve the tenor of our politics.

These are big projects. Do we have enough energy remaining for this sort of thing?

What is it to our souls when we have to just keep slugging through dark places? Why, after all that has happened in America, from stolen elections to the destruction of our necessary institutions of mutual help, are you activists still at it? Why, after seeing our country become the international symbol of irresponsible conduct, of torture, of political imprisonment, of destruction to the global ecosystem, are your spirits not smeared across the plaza under the treads of these tanks?

Are your hearts perhaps stronger and your souls deeper than you imagined? Yes, this is what you came here to do. There is no greater gift than to be given a life of meaning. There is no greater heroism than to bravely represent love in a dark time of fear and danger.

We are resolved to help each other. We are resolved to represent love in the world and to follow our national dream.

So, look at the situation wisely and know that a good ending is not to be found under the paper moon of child's brief play. Accept and celebrate the fact that we are deeply engaged in a long, hard drama of global meaning. We welcome the fight. We welcome it, and, by George Washington, we are up to it.

Thank you.

Last Delivered Speech

> *Ms. Haddock was honored on January 24, 2010, her 100th birthday, in the chambers of New Hampshire's governor. Several hundred attended. Her thank you remarks were her last delivered speech:*

Thank you all so very, very much. That you would take time from your busy lives to be here is a great gift to me, and I thank you for it. People have been asking me how I feel about the recent decision by the Supreme Court to strike down some of the campaign finance reforms that I walked for and have been working on for a dozen or so years.

When I was a young woman, my husband and I were having dinner at the Dundee home of a friend, Max Foster, when a young couple rushed through the door breathless to say that they had accidentally burned down the guest cabin down by the river. Max stood up from his meal. He set his napkin down. He smiled at the young couple and he said:

"That's wonderful. We have wanted to build something special down there on the river, and this will give us a chance to do that without feeling guilty about getting rid of that drafty old thing."

Well, I guess the Supreme Court has burned down our little cabin, but, truth be told, it was pretty drafty anyway. We had not really solved the problem of too much money in politics, and now we have an opportunity to start clean and build a system of reforms that really will do the trick.

Thank you all, very much indeed for coming here, for the cake, my little crown, and for absolutely everything.

The Swamp to Drain is Anger (undelivered)

Her last prepared speech went undelivered. It was meant for the September 11, 2010 Fighting Bob (La Follette) Fest in Wisconsin, an annual gathering of national reformers. Her death intervening, Ms. Haddock was able to attend in spirit only.

Thank you very much. Nations, more than their boundaries or resources or wealth, are a mental condition. A nation may be open and positive, hard-working and fully confident of its future. It may send great white fleets around the world and humans into space. A nation may also be angry, self-destructive and cruel.

We are individuals and we are parts of a whole. The whole can be as troubled or as ecstatic and positive as its individuals. You all know this very well, and you know that, at the present time, America is angry and divided and mentally disturbed. Many of its citizens are turning away from obvious truths and embracing angry and dangerous fantasies.

If someone you know flies off the handle in an uncharacteristic way and will not listen to the clear facts, perhaps his dear wife will take you aside and explain that there is a major problem in the family to account for the outburst. It's hard to settle arguments and put away anger when we are desperately anxious about our future and our family. That sort of anxiety is driving America's politics today. Where does it come from? Anger and blindness to the facts are the children of powerlessness—powerlessness over one's own and one's family's future.

That anxiety is manipulated by self-interested grandmasters. In the 1950s, as great corporations began to wash away the family businesses of Main Street and as the new interstate highways destroyed the economics of a million small towns, the anger of those middle-class families should have been directed against those corporations and the political officials in league with them. Instead, the anger was purposely and methodically redirected against a nearly phantom Communist threat inside America, against the civil rights of blacks, and against any expansion of government into worker protection, environmental protection and consumer protection. Because the anxiety was misdirected, it was not brought to bear on the proper cause of the anxiety, and so the anxiety only grew.

Corporations and the very wealthiest people began to finance the election campaigns of their foot soldiers in Congress. They financed talk radio and propaganda cable television. In 1987, they destroyed the Fairness Doctrine in broadcast news programs. We now see millions of people whose anxiety has been hijacked and redirected against their own best interests.

In the Reagan years, all the stops were taken off things like hostile corporate takeovers and the rise of new monopolies, so that even the most ethical companies were forced to ship their jobs overseas and shutter their plants in American towns and cities to avoid hostile takeovers. This was all very profitable for the wealthiest elite. You might wonder why these people have allowed things to go so far that the Earth of their grandchildren is now endangered—perhaps fatally, and the answer is that they do not care about their children or grandchildren, so long as they themselves can buy the longest yachts at the Monaco yacht show. How embarrassing it must be if their checkbooks are unable to do so—perhaps as embarrassing as it is for a single mother whose bankcard is declined at the grocery store.

From those yachts are sent instructions that control what Fox News watchers and talk radio listeners will be upset about tomorrow. These abused and misinformed people will be used to stop all real progress toward real solutions, and the mass anxiety of the people will grow even greater, even as their homes are taken from them and their foods are poisoned and the climate warms to boiling for their grandchildren.

All this opinion engineering needs ready enemies, and so it is the Mexican immigrants or the Arabs or Muslims or any other Others will have the honor of being scapegoats and diversions. We could, after all, stop illegal immigration by improving economic conditions in Latin America, and we could end Arab anger by moving our economy from oil to solar, but those are big business considerations for proper discussion in the yachts off Monaco, not in our pretend Congress. The yachts off Monaco are sending no sons and daughters to the oil wars—at least no sons and daughters that they really care about.

So, the anger of anxiety grows. Guns and ammunition now flow into our communities in semi-trucks for gun shows. The politics polarizes to the extent that some have no moral or patriotic objection to sabotaging the economy if it will mean more votes in the next election. And facts as plain as day—as plain as a birth certificate—will be insulted and burned in the streets.

Some years ago, a dam gave way in Buffalo Creek in West Virginia, sending billions of gallons of toxic coal sludge down into a valley, where it destroyed towns and killed many people. That lake of sludge grew over the years behind that insufficient dam as corrupt inspectors signed reports and mines lied and continued to send sludge higher and higher. You can think of American anger in the same way, rising from the lies and failures to represent and the destruction of the middle class and its businesses and the loss of power that people sense over their own futures. When the dam goes, democracy will be hard to pull alive from the sludge. It will be very difficult. We will do it, of course, but it will be very difficult, and people will have died.

If I were the President of the United States looking at all this, what would I do now?

I would do a great deal.

I would use administrative powers to do as much as I could to return a sense of personal power to people. Every notch will help defuse anger. I would require federally insured banks to have human beings answer their phones, and have local human beings assigned to personally help every customer, with full authority to make most decisions regarding those accounts.

I would find out in which other industries federal leverage might permit similar returns to the human scale, so that people had more daily moments when they did not feel so powerless against the machinery of modern life.

As the President, I would look at the companies that sell things to the federal government. I would give a purchasing preference to those companies that dumped their computerized, outsourced telephone systems and other systems of human contact in favor of a more human-scaled operation.

I would give a thousand preferences to small businesses. I would even subsidize small businesses directly, maybe funded by a heavy wealth tax on billionaires. I would order the agencies of government to buy American products when possible, even at a premium, and especially from smaller businesses.

Without turning my back on the environment or on worker rights and safety, I would start a campaign against the kinds of red tape that inhibit the creation of Main Street businesses and small-scale manufacturers. The object of these moves would be simple: to give more people a sense of control over their own lives and futures.

I expect a roomful of citizens could come up with a thousand things that make them feel disempowered and that might be changed. Little empowerments can build toward more meaningful power. People ultimately need to believe, and correctly so, that their daily efforts will bear the harvest they have earned.

We need to get rid of the anger created by all kinds of financial debt borne by young people and old. When we owned the banks after the 2008 crash, we should have ripped up the loans. Why the hell didn't we? We still need to do it, because the stresses become anger and the anger is eating up our country.

And little things add up: All the fine print in contracts—you shouldn't have to sign a ten-page contract to listen to a song or share a family photo. All those little things are insulting to us, and they add up. Maybe we will need to take our shoes off at the airport for a while yet, but we shouldn't have to bow so low to every company that tells us to.

Stores ought to look for shoplifters and stop them, but devices that scan and beep at the doorways, and clerks who stop you at the door before leaving to examine your basket and your receipt are making an accusation that you are probably a thief, and Americans should not be accusing each other of such things without probable cause. It is dehumanizing. Our dignity demands a presumption of innocence not only in the courts but in our daily lives.

These little things that eat away at our dignity ultimately make us angry and alienated. So, end those practices. Put consumer and government pressure to bear to make companies comply with a new golden rule of personal treatment in America. When people are treated with an expectation of honor, they tend to respond. The few that do not are not worth worrying about.

We need to do something about our middle and high schools, which are factories of alienation and stress. Let's do that first. We don't need Congress for that.

And when we do have a Congress that again represents the people, we need to return to the states the authority to limit interest rates that can be charged on loans and credit cards. States once had that power, and rates were generally limited to not much over ten percent; but then the interstate banking lobby purchased Congress and we are all now paying for their yachts as a result. Let's make this a states' rights issue and confuse the far right.

The United States of America has an interest in the development of small, family-run local and regional businesses. Those businesses are good for the economy, good for communities, good for families, good for personal empowerment, and good for democracy. When we have a real Congress again, lets create a corporate tax system that discourages businesses from growing larger than they need to be. A computer company or an automobile company or an aircraft company may need to be large, but there is no reason for general merchandise stores to be overlarge. There is no reason for insurance companies or media companies to be overlarge. Returning the economy to a more local and more human scale is important and necessary for our political, cultural and ecological health.

While we are at it, we should get rid of corporate-run prisons. What is a greater insult to an American than to be locked up by a corporation? Anyone in that circumstance ought to have a right to resist. It insults all of us. If we fail to act on these matters, the sense of personal disempowerment will grow, and also its anger and its violence.

Returning a more human scale to our economy would also create quite a few jobs and quite a few new businesses. If a U.S. president would take up an aggressive campaign to return human scale and its personal power to Americans, I don't think he or she would find too many opponents, except in the yachts off Monaco. They would of course instruct Fox News to rail against this return to the Stone Age. But the anger that fuels their toxic enterprise and others like it would dissipate, and we might soon have a governable country again.

The idea of a social safety net, while constantly attacked by the wealthy elite and their followers, provide important ways to reduce the kinds of anxiety that otherwise disrupt society and democracy. If parents know their children will be able to attend college without debt, that they themselves will have a secure old age, and that the only time people will sleep outdoors in America is when they are camping, then they will be better neighbors, better parents, better spouses, better and more productive workers, and better Americans.

If there is one thing that would guarantee any President's election or re-election, it is this final suggestion: A President could administratively modify the procurement code of the federal government so that companies that do not lobby the federal government in any way except in open hearings are eligible for federal contracts worth over a million dollars. Otherwise, they aren't eligible.

This political disempowerment of corporations would result in a grand re-empowerment of average citizens, who then would stand a chance being heard by their elected representatives.

With every notch—and that would be a big one—anger subsides, racism subsides, we step away from the precipice now before us, and we move toward a much better America.

These are ideas someone might package and promote. A joining of left and right might be possible regarding elements of this package. A president or presidential candidate might even listen.

Frankly, I don't think we have much time to waste.

Anger is what is in our way, and it comes from the disempowerment of us all, and from the alienation that results from disempowerment.

Thank you very much, and God bless the memory of Bob La Follette.

Senator Russ Feingold, Senate Floor, Oct. 14, 1999

Mr. President, we have some momentum. I was delighted this week to have us get another cosponsor on this bill, the Senator from Kansas, SAM BROWNBACK, and to also have the endorsement of one of the leaders from the other body, Congressman Asa Hutchinson. So we have had good momentum this week. I am pleased with that. I especially felt the momentum when last Friday I had a chance to go to Nashville, Tennessee, and I had the good fortune to meet an extraordinary woman, who is in Washington today. I'm speaking of Doris Haddock, from Dublin, New Hampshire. Doris has become known to many people throughout the country and around the world as ``Granny D.''

She is 89 years old. On January 1st of this year, she set out to walk across this country to call attention to the need for campaign finance reform and call on this body to pass the McCain-Feingold bill. As she said last week, voting for McCain-Feingold is something our mothers and grandmothers would want us to do. And coming from Granny D, this is not just a polite request--it is a challenge and a demand from one of the toughest and bravest advocates of reform I have ever had the pleasure to know.

I joined Granny D on the road last week, and as we walked together through the streets of Nashville, shouts of ``Go Granny Go'' came from every corner--from drivers in their cars, pedestrians on the sidewalk and construction workers on the job.
The response she got that day, and the support she gets every day on her walk across America, speak volumes about where the American people stand on this issue. They are fed up with a campaign finance system so clogged with cash that it has essentially ceased to function; they are frustrated by a Congress that has stood by and watched our democracy deteriorate; and today they are demanding that the U.S. Senate join Granny D on the road to reform by passing the McCain-Feingold bill.

Granny D and countless Americans like her are demanding, here and now, that this body act to ban soft money and begin to clean up our campaign finance mess. Granny has been walking across this country for more than nine months now--from California to Tennessee, in the sweltering heat and now in the growing cold, over mountains and across a desert. At age 89, she has braved all of this. And all she is asking U.S. Senators to do in return one simple thing.

What she's asking is not anywhere near as strenuous, and it won't take anywhere near as much time as what she has endured. All she is asking the members of this body to do is lift their arm to cast one vote--a vote to ban soft money.

That's what she's asking, and I urge my colleagues not let her down. The time is past for the excuses, equivocations and evasions that members of this body have employed time and again to avoid passing campaign finance reform legislation. The time has come to put partisanship aside, to put our own ideal reform bills aside and finally put our democracy first--let's join Granny D on the road to reform.

I yield the floor.

Senate Concurrent Resolution 58 - Recognizing Doris "Granny D" Haddock, who inspired millions of people through remarkable acts of political activism, and extending the condolences of Congress on the death of Doris "Granny D" Haddock. 111th Congress (2009-2010)

www.ingramcontent.com/pod-product-compliance
Lightning Source LLC
Chambersburg PA
CBHW041617220426
43671CB00004B/45